© Rudy Gelenter

About the Author

John Baxter has lived in Paris for more than twenty
years. He is the author of three acclaimed memoirs about
his life in France: *The Most Beautiful Walk in the World:
A Pedestrian in Paris*; *Immoveable Feast: A Paris Christmas*; and *We'll Always Have Paris: Sex and Love in the
City of Light*. Baxter, who gives literary walking tours
through Paris, is also a film critic and biographer whose
subjects have included the directors Fellini, Kubrick,
Woody Allen, and most recently, Josef von Sternberg.
Born in Australia, he lives with his wife and daughter in
the Saint-Germain-des-Prés neighborhood, in the same
building Sylvia Beach called home.

The
PERFECT
MEAL

Also by John Baxter

The Most Beautiful Walk in the World

Von Sternberg

Carnal Knowledge

Immoveable Feast

We'll Always Have Paris

A Pound of Paper

Science Fiction in the Cinema

The Cinema of Josef von Sternberg

Buñuel

Fellini

Stanley Kubrick

Steven Spielberg

Woody Allen

George Lucas

Robert DeNiro

Translated by John Baxter

My Lady Opium by Claude Farrère

Morphine by Jean-Louis Dubut de Laforest

The Diary of a Chambermaid by Octave Mirbeau

Gamiani, or Two Night of Excess by Alfred de Musset

The

PERFECT
MEAL

In Search of the Lost
Tastes of France

John Baxter

HARPER ⬤ PERENNIAL

NEW YORK • LONDON • TORONTO • SYDNEY • NEW DELHI • AUCKLAND

HARPER ● PERENNIAL

HarperCollins books may be purchased for educational, business, or sales
promotional use. For information please write: Special Markets Department,
HarperCollins Publishers, 10 East 53rd Street, New York, NY 10022.

FIRST EDITION

Designed by Michael Correy

Library of Congress Cataloging-in-Publication Data is available upon request.

ISBN 978-0-06-208806-2

13 14 15 16 17   OV/RRD   10 9 8 7 6 5 4 3 2 1

For Marie-Dominique and Louise, who taught me
that cooking is all about love, and for Georges
Auguste Escoffier, who kept the faith

Tell me what you eat, and I shall tell you what you are.

Jean Anthelme Brillat-Savarin, French gastronome

Contents

The

PERFECT
MEAL

One

First Catch Your Pansy

I've taken to cooking and listening to Wagner, both of which frighten me to death.

Noël Coward, diary entry, Sunday, February 19, 1956

It all began with the pansy in my soup.

Rick Gekoski was in town, so we went out to dinner. Rick deals in rare books, but only the rarest. He's sold first editions of *Lolita* to rock stars, bought J. R. R. Tolkien's bathrobe, and so charmed Graham Greene that the great writer let him purchase the library in his Antibes apartment. In between, he's written a few books and chaired the panel presenting the Booker Prize, Britain's most prestigious literary award.

After the Greene deal, the two men shared an aperitif in the café below Greene's home.

"Y'know," said Greene, "if I hadn't been a writer, I'd have liked to do what you do—be a bookseller."

For a man who could excite the envy of a literary giant, no ordinary meal would suffice.

"Have you eaten at the Grand Palais?" I asked Rick.

"You mean that block-long example of Belle Époque bad taste just off the Champs-Élysées?" he asked. "I've attended art fairs and book fairs there. I'm told it also hosts automobile shows, horse shows, and I believe once accommodated a trade show for manufacturers of farm machinery. But eaten there? Never."

"A new experience, then."

In 1993 the Grand Palais shut down for renovations. Fragments of the 8,500-ton glass-and-steel roof showed an alarming tendency to fall on unsuspecting heads. To keep the building at least partly alive, the terrace along one side became the Minipalais restaurant, with triple-Michelin-star chef Eric Frechon in charge. I'd enjoyed some pleasant meals there, as much for the setting as the food. I hoped Rick might be impressed.

The following evening, we mounted the wide steps at the corner of avenue Winston Churchill.

The Grand Palais is the kind of building that takes the eye. More vast than an aircraft hangar, it soared above our heads. Along one side, the 65-foot-high columns of the terrace dwindled into the dusk. The marble-floored foyer would have done credit to an imperial embassy. Even Rick conceded a respectful "Humph."

While we waited to be seated, I looked across the avenue at the statue of Britain's wartime prime minister after whom it was named. Churchill leaned on his stick and glared, as if remembering his problems with Charles de Gaulle when the Free French government in exile fled to London in 1940.

Anyone who knew the eating habits of the two men could have foreseen they would never get on. Churchill was a drinker, de Gaulle an eater, or at least someone who embraced the philosophy of "Devour, or be devoured." Metaphors about food pepper his writings. Dismissing the idea of a Communist France, he inquired, "How can any one party govern a nation that has two hundred and forty-six different kinds of cheese?" (In fact, there are more like 350.) Asked about his literary "influences," de Gaulle scorned the suggestion that any other mind might affect his thinking. "A lion is made up of the lambs he's digested." But in Churchill, as gifted a writer, orator, and statesman as he, he'd met another lion, and the two men snarled over the future of Europe like two males over the same kill.

The waitress led us into the dining room, quarried from the Palais's mezzanine, and tried to seat us at one of its tables.

"I asked for a table on the terrace," I said.

She gave one of the *moues* for which the French mouth is uniquely constructed.

"*Mes excuses, monsieur.* Were you actually *guaranteed* a table on the terrace?"

"Well . . . no . . ."

Her shoulders started to rise in that other French specialty, the shrug that indicates powerlessness in the face of overwhelming contrary circumstances. (Interestingly, there is no single French word for "shrug." Asked to define it, a French person will just . . . well, shrug.)

"After dinner," Rick interjected, "I intend to enjoy a cigar."

Dipping into an inside pocket, he extracted an aluminum tube the length of a torpedo. The family that would have been seated next to us leaned away collectively. They knew the smoke generated by a weed that size could entirely obscure their dessert.

"I will see what I can do," the waitress said hurriedly.

Two minutes later we were seated on the terrace, under those soaring columns, looking out on the gathering darkness and the Seine flowing in stately complacency beneath the Pont Alexandre III. In 1919 a triumphant General Pershing, on horseback, led Ameri-

British soldiers parade past the Grand Palais, 1916

can troops on a victory parade along the avenue below us while cheering Parisians crowded the space where we sat and flung flowers. We were in the presence of history.

"So . . ." Rick pocketed his cigar and reached for the carte. "How's the food here?"

Twenty minutes later, my first course arrived.

Marooned in the middle of an otherwise empty soup plate was a small mound of something green and granular—peas mashed with mint, I later discovered. It supported two tiny slices of white asparagus, so thin I could have read *Le Monde* through them—and the small print at that.

"I ordered the cold asparagus soup."

"This *will be* the asparagus soup, m'sieur," said the waiter.

He returned with an aluminum CO_2 bottle, from which he squirted white froth around the peas. A few seconds later, he was back with a jug from which he poured a milky liquid—the first thing to resemble soup.

"*Voilà, m'sieur. Votre Soupe d'asperge Blanche, Mousseline de Petit Pois à la Menthe Fraîche. Bon appétit.*"

Belatedly, I noticed the finishing touch on top of the peas and asparagus.

It was a tiny pansy.

"There's a pansy in my soup."

Close to midnight, we strolled across the bridge in the soft Paris night. I thought I could still smell Rick's cigar, which, when he did fire it up over coffee and calvados, was only one of many being enjoyed on the terrace. Their smoke rose into the shadows at the top of the treelike columns. Statues looked down in approval. For a moment, surrounded by the architecture of a heroic age, we had felt ourselves, if not gods, then at least priests of some hallowed rite, celebrating the joys of food and drink.

If it hadn't been for that pansy.

"A place like that . . ." Rick said as we walked.

He looked back over his shoulder at the line of columns marching in majesty toward the Champs-Élysées.

"Not that the food wasn't good . . ."

And it had been good. Just a bit . . . well, precious.

The ingredients and dishes were, on paper at least, traditional: pork belly, snails, even a burger. But the pork, instead of arriving rich and fat, sizzling from the barbecue, proved to be a severe oblong, glossy and sharp-edged. Posed on a heap of boiled potatoes lightly crushed with grain mustard, it resembled Noah's ark aground on Mount Ararat. For *Escargots dans Leur Tomate Cerise Gratinés au Beurre d'Amande*, a dozen snails were embedded, for no very good reason, in individual cherry tomatoes, and the whole dish was covered in a gratin of butter and powdered almonds. Least likely of all, the "burger" was a nugget of duck breast in a tiny bun, topped with foie gras and drizzled with truffle juice. At the sight of it, Ronald McDonald would have fainted dead away .

"I know what you mean," I said. "With that décor, you expect something . . . imperial."

A vision rose of a meal appropriate to such architecture. It was straight out of a Hollywood epic such as *Ben-Hur* or *Gladiator*. Dressed in togas, we and the other customers reclined on couches, nibbling bunches of grapes. Lightly dressed concubines danced among us. And in the background, a team of sweating slaves turned a spit on which roasted an entire ox.

But who cooked on that scale anymore? What had happened to the robust country dishes of fifty years ago, before the advent of nouvelle cuisine and food designed not to satisfy hunger but to show off the imagination of the chef? Did they still exist? Or were they, as I suspected, lost forever, the secret of their making having died with the last country chef who still remembered the recipe handed down to him or her through generations. Even if someone still knew how to prepare them, where would they find the ingredients? Modern markets stocked only what they could pile high and sell fast.

Specifically, did anyone still really roast an ox?

Two

First Catch Your Menu

In France, cooking is a serious art form and a national sport.

Julia Child

Anglo-Saxon countries accept that fantasies con-
ceived over dinner evaporate before the next
morning's coffee, passing, like New Year's resolutions,
from the world of What If to that of If Only.

Fortunately, the French keep a little ajar the door into
that universe of tantalizing alternatives. They speak of
actions being *envisagées*—not ruled out, not impossible,
perhaps not likely to happen in the immediate future, but
contemplated; envisaged.

Then there's *l'esprit d'escalier*—"the inspiration of
the staircase." These are the thoughts that occur as you
descend the stairs after a dinner party; the riposte that
would have reduced a bore to incoherence; the compliment that, had you thought of it at the time, would have

caused your partner to slip you her phone number under the table. Rather than waste such fertile second thoughts, French literature invented the *pensée*, strictly speaking a collection of thoughts, aphorisms, anecdotes, and reflections, but actually a means of putting on paper all those zingers that would otherwise have faded into the air.

All the same, my idea of a fabulous banquet, like any product of late-night indigestion and the gleam of the moon on the Seine, might have dissipated in the same way, except for a report in the next day's issue of *Le Monde*. The intergovernmental committee of UNESCO had declared the formal French dinner, or *repas*, an element of humanity's "intangible cultural heritage."

Two years before, President Nicolas Sarkozy had announced at an agricultural fair that French cuisine was the best in the world and should be acknowledged as such. It's the kind of thing politicians say to placate a powerful lobby, and in France few carry more weight than agribusiness.

But apparently the European Institute of History and Culture of Food, a uniquely French institution (try to conceive an American version), had been busy lobbying behind the scenes. Meeting in Nairobi, a twenty-four-member panel from UNESCO considered forty-seven nominations but singled out the "gastronomic meal of the French" as worthy of preservation, not just for the edification of the French—who needed no convincing—but also for the good of the human race.

UNESCO laid down rules to define the classic *repas*—something no French authority had ever dared do, knowing it would immediately be attacked by every other French authority in the world of food.

The gastronomic meal should respect a fixed structure, commencing with an apéritif (drinks before the meal) and ending with liqueurs, containing in between at least four successive courses, namely a starter, fish and/or meat with vegetables, cheese and dessert. Individuals called gastronomes who possess deep knowledge of the tradition and preserve its memory watch over the living practice of the rites, thus contributing to their oral and/or written transmission, in particular to younger generations.

To share such a meal with family and friends did more than satisfy hunger. It was, decreed the committee, "a social practice designed to celebrate the most important moments in the lives of individuals and groups."

To me, it seemed a classic case of shutting the stable door after the horse had bolted. Who ate like this anymore, least of all in the big cities of France? A feast of eight to ten courses, with wine, for anything up to twenty people, would cost a fortune, even at home. In a restaurant, the cost would be dizzying, even assuming the chef and serving staff were equal

to the challenge. Restaurants no longer catered for large parties; their ovens were too small to roast a whole sucking pig, a haunch of venison, a side of beef. Most relied on microwaves or resorted to warming up precooked dishes bought in cans or boil-in-a-bag portions.

Then there were the foibles of the diners to be considered: no fat, no sugar, no salt. Vegetarian, vegan, kosher, halal. . . . The modern chef faced a minefield, which he was happy to avoid by cooking only those dishes that risked giving no offense. The difficult disappeared.

Following the announcement, a certain amount of muttering was heard in the cooking communities of other countries. Weren't the culinary traditions of Germany, Britain, even America, also worth celebrating?

French cooks grudgingly conceded that perhaps the banquets of America's Thanksgiving or the British Christmas were not without their pleasures. Between France and Germany, however, too much bad blood existed for the latter's cooking ever to be taken seriously.

This ill will went back to the middle of the nine-teenth century, before the states of the future Germany were united. When Prussia and France went to war in 1870, the man who would become France's greatest chef, Georges-Auguste Escoffier, was called up, was captured, and endured almost a year of misery in a German prison camp, existing on undercooked beans and lentils, wormy pork, and rotten potatoes. He emerged with a loathing of German food.

In 1913, Kaiser Wilhelm II asked him to organize a lunch for 146 people on the liner *Imperator* as it launched a transatlantic service from Hamburg to New York. In his memoirs, Escoffier doesn't hide his bitterness at the way he was treated by the Kaiser. First, he had to convince Wilhelm's staff that his imprisonment wouldn't tempt him to poison the Kaiser. They still demanded a German version of the menu, so that each dish could be checked. It included a *Mousse d'Écrevisse*—a chilled mold of crayfish. *Mousse*, however, can also mean "cabin boy," and the translator demanded indignantly if the chef really believed Germans were sufficiently monstrous to devour the crew.

The day after the dinner, the Kaiser sent for Escoffier and reportedly told him, "I am the Emperor of Germany, but you are the Emperor of Chefs." Although this was the most famous compliment he ever received, Escoffier doesn't mention it in his memoirs, making only the terse comment "Hardly one year after this brilliant reception, Germany declared war on France. On November 1, 1914, my son Daniel, lieutenant in the 363rd Alpine Regiment, was hit full in the face by a Prussian bullet and died instantly, leaving his four children for me to bring up."

The Sunday after our dinner at the Minipalais, I spent the morning at a *brocante* in Montmartre.

Brocante—derivation unknown, or at least much wrangled over—can mean either the secondhand goods sold in a market or the market itself, or even a shop that stocks such things. *Brocantes* and *vide-greniers* are a feature of French life—increasingly so as the French realize the value of recycling.

In Paris, the year-round markets at Porte de Vanves and Porte Clignancourt are cornucopias of junk that contain the occasional treasure. As the weather warms, others erupt all over France, invading public squares, school parking lots, suburban streets. Outside Paris, they often sprout in a field or around the village football pitch.

Brocanteurs

In this case, the stalls straggled down the tree-shaded central island of rue de Rochechouart, in the north of Paris, on the slopes of Montmartre. As I browsed those set out under the trees, a stream of tourists bubbled up from the Envers metro station, paled at the slope confronting them, and, hitching their backpacks higher on their shoulders like weary mountaineers, began the final ascent to the mushroom-gray domes of the cathedral of Sacré-Coeur crouched on the summit.

My eye was caught by a pile of heavy earthenware dishes sitting on the pavement, half-hidden in crumpled newspaper. Their gray-white surfaces were crazed with *craquelure*, the web of tiny cracks that indicate age, while the underside of each had been glazed a lustrous black in the style the French call, with typical directness, *cul noir*— "black ass." Similar lead-glazed dishes and pots exist in Mexico, Japan, and Poland, some dating back to the eighteenth century, but these were almost certainly made in Brittany late in the nineteenth. I'd seen similar plates in antique stores, displayed in glass cases, with prices to match.

Rule one of *brocantes*, particularly if one is a foreigner, is to hide your interest. Spotting a dusty plastic sandwich bag filled with old documents, I dropped it into the top dish and held them out to the bored young man drowsing in the hot morning sun.

"Combien?" I asked.

He stared blankly at my finds, then craned to look over the heads of the crowd. Obviously this wasn't his stall. But his boss, like every other *exposant*, was trolling for bargains in the stock of his competitors.

Finally he said, "Um, *dix?*"

Was that ten for each item or for the lot? I didn't let him think about it. He stared for a moment at the ten-euro note I shoved in his hand, then made that half shrug that only the French have mastered. Ten euros for some old dishes and a few papers? It sounded fair—and it was too hot to haggle.

•   •   •

B ack home, I wiped the dust off one of the dishes, arranged three crimson Jonathan apples on it, and placed it on the dining room table, where it caught the sun slanting through the wooden shutters. Beat that, Henri Matisse.

Almost as an afterthought, I emptied out the documents. Most were menus: a dozen or more, all from around 1911 or 1912, the majority for private dinners to celebrate a first communion, a retirement, or a wedding.

A few were meticulously hand-lettered. One could imagine the steel-nib pen dipped in a ceramic inkpot. Nothing else could achieve the rich downward curve of the *S* in *Salade* or that tail, called a serif, on the *P* of *Poulet*—a trick of penmanship and printing seen only in cultures where the eye, untrained in reading, needs to be led. Others were formally printed on heavy stock, with a flowery heading, the word *Menu* flanked by game birds, lobsters, fish, flowers, and fruit. And rightly so, since what these ancient cards trumpeted most flagrantly was not only tradition and ritual but excess.

One card, headed simply "15 April 1912"—almost exactly a century ago—outlined a formal lunch.

This was the kind of meal UNESCO had in mind. But where were such meals made today? These were truly "lost" dishes. For the modern cook, even the culinary language would be baffling.

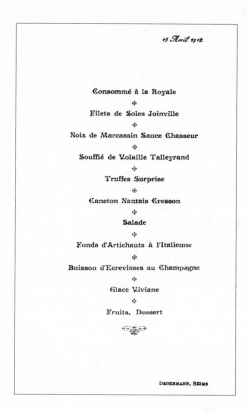

15 Avril 1918.

Consommé à la Royale
✣
Filets de Soles Joinville
✣
Noix de Marcassin Sauce Chasseur
✣
Soufflé de Volaille Talleyrand
✣
Truffes Surprise
✣
Caneton Nantais Cresson
✣
Salade
✣
Fonds d'Artichauts à l'Italienne
✣
Buisson d'Ecrevisses au Champagne
✣
Glace Viviane
✣
Fruits, Dessert

DEGERMANN, REIMS

To deserve the description *Royale*, for example, a dish required a rich additional ingredient, making it "fit for a king." But it's been many years since any chef made a serious effort to achieve regal status for his work, and the few attempts have been dismal. In 1953 a competition for a new dish to mark the crowning of Queen Elizabeth produced Coronation Chicken, a lumpy mixture of chopped chicken in curry-flavored mayonnaise. No sooner was the recipe published than someone pointed out an embarrassing resemblance to the Jubilee Chicken created for George V's Golden Jubilee in 1935, also using curry mayonnaise. Obviously news of neither dish reached the people charged with creating something for the 2012 Jubilee of Queen Elizabeth, since they came up with . . . yes, chopped chicken in spicy mayonnaise.

Making *Consommé à la Royale* in 1912, the chef would have beaten eggs with cream, poured the mixture into molds, poached it, then cut the omelette-like solid into strips. Placing a few of these in a soup bowl with thin slices of chicken breast, mushroom, and truffle, he'd have ladled hot chicken consommé on top. Not something to be knocked up in a few minutes for unexpected guests.

For *Noix de Marcassin Sauce Chasseur*, filets from a young boar, or *marcassin*, were sautéed in butter, then served in a sauce of white wine, butter, and herbs. To create a *buisson*, or bush, of *écrivisses*, the chef arranged shelled crayfish in a pyramid, on a base of champagne aspic. For *Soufflé de Volaille Talleyrand*, chicken breasts were pounded into a paste and folded into the egg mixture before the soufflé went into the oven.

In 1912 even a modest provincial restaurant might have handled such a meal, with a little advance notice. But we live in an era when an average restaurant has two or three cooks rather than ten, and one of those an apprentice. Technology takes up the slack. In the wholesale supermarkets that ring Paris, reserved for the trade, the chefs of Paris's best restaurants trundle six-wheeled steel platforms rather than shopping carts, and arrive at the checkouts with sacks of frozen *frites*, five-portion cans of *confit de canard*, and cartons of ready-to-reheat *chicken à la crème*, *boeuf bourguignon*, and *blanquette de veau*. In 2011, two thirds of French restaurants admitted to using *plats en kit*—precooked meals bought canned, frozen, or as boil-in-a-bag portions.

Anything from the menu of 1912 that can't be cooked in a microwave or under a grill has disappeared. As soufflés must be made on the spot, *Soufflé de Volaille Talleyrand* would appear only in the rare restaurants that specialize in them. But frozen or canned artichoke hearts have saved *Fonds d'Artichauts à l'Italienne*, and *Caneton Nantais Cresson* may survive, because every joint of the duck is available precooked, complete with sauce. Just add some sprigs of fresh watercress and serve.

•   •   •

Markets, too, have been transformed. Of my local shopping streets, rue de Buci and rue de Seine, a visitor of the 1950s wrote that they were:

> *always buzzing, lined with vegetable pushcarts both sides, meat and fish stores behind them, invariably thronged with shoppers. Walking through it, one was knocked over by the stench of rotten cabbage leaves, fresh turnips, raw tripe, steers' red blood. Early morning, and the fire hydrants spurting, turned on by the street cleaners; the murky waters rolling over the ancient cobblestones; up wafting the odor of stale wine, Gauloises butts, spermatozoa, Lysol; running a few blocks down to the Quai des Grands-Augustins and the Seine, flowing soft and serene as an angel's sigh.*

He wouldn't recognize them now. The fishmongers and cheese sellers have long gone. One forlorn relic remains. Next to the Hotel Louisiane, over a permanently shuttered shop front, black tiles on a blue background spell out the word *Poissonerie*. The blue is the color of the Greek flag; the color James Joyce dictated for the cover of the first edition of *Ulysses*, published just a few blocks away, at Sylvia Beach's Shakespeare and Company. Joyce walked down this street a hundred times. Did he look up one day, see the tiles, and make a mental note? The lightning of inspiration can strike anywhere.

That phantom fish shop will never reopen, nor will rue Buci ever again stink from stale wine and semen. The space belongs to Italian gelato parlors, *chocolatiers*, wine merchants, shops selling organic cosmetics, and, of course, cafés, which each year extend their wooden platforms a little farther into the street, the better to squeeze in more tables.

As for pushcarts, they would impede the view of the tourists who sip their *cafés crèmes* at those tables. Occasionally a street vendor of the old school reappears for a morning, like a ghost of another era. Once it was a car from the 1920s, lacquered a funereal black, with a gleaming brass hood ornament and wheel hubs, and the back half-converted to hold tubs of homemade ice cream.

The ice cream seller

Also, periodically, the sidewalk in front of the butcher is colonized by two dour men selling wrinkled dry sausage; wheels of hard cheese with thick, gnarled rind; and wind-dried hams from the mountainous and heavily forested part of central France known as the Auvergne. Though the sellers' wide-brimmed black hats and black cotton smocks look a little like fancy dress, they are authentic enough, as are their products. Taking American visitors on a stroll one Saturday, I paused by their stall to enumerate the ingredients of their salami-like *saucissons secs*: "*saucisson d'sanglier* . . . sausage of wild boar; *saucisson de noix* . . . sausage with walnuts; *saucisson d'âne* . . ." I paused, glancing at my friends. Would they want to know that the next sausage was made from donkey meat? Probably not.

L ong after that dinner at the Grand Palais, memories of it continued to circulate in my mind.

Of course, one couldn't actually duplicate the Roman feast I'd visualized. Who, for instance, any longer roasted oxen? Did oxen even exist? An ox was what Americans call a steer, a castrated bull. In Europe and Asia, the castration made them more tractable to pull a cart or a plough, neither much used these days.

Was there, somewhere in France, even a vestige of the food culture represented by that classical architecture and by the menu of 1912? If so, where was it hiding? Might there even be, in some remote corner of the country, an ox waiting to be roasted and the people who knew how to perform this medieval rite?

It would be fun to find out: to create, even in imagination, the kind of feast UNESCO decided was typical of French cuisine. But I needed an inspiration, a spark, a guide.

Fortunately, I had Boris.

Three

First Catch Your Mentor

I could undertake to be an efficient pupil if it were possible to find an efficient teacher.

Gertrude Stein

In a movie of the 1980s—title forgotten, if ever known—a woman, chef in a rural restaurant somewhere in the south of France, has just prepared lunch for twenty obviously important men.

They praise her skill, particularly the main dish. Such a sauce! Never have they eaten better. She has exceeded herself.

She returns to the kitchen, where the pot remains on the stove. For a long moment she stares at it. Then, ladling out a few spoonsful into a dish, she carries it to the back door. Sitting on the steps outside, an old man in an open shirt and ragged trousers is peeling potatoes. She holds out the dish.

"Would you mind tasting this?"

Dropping the last potato into a bucket of water, he wipes his hands on his trousers. Taking the dish and spoon, he tastes. He ponders, but not for long.

"What wine did you use?" he asks.

Instantly, the cook slumps. "I knew it! All the '49 had gone, so I had to use some of the '50."

He hands back the dish. "Ah, well, there you are, then," he says sympathetically, but with an edge of reproof. No need to rub in the fact that, by the harsh standards only they share, she has failed.

I saw this film years ago, but nothing has shaken my awe for the conviction at its heart: that there are people of such discrimination that they have forgotten more than you and I will ever know about how things should taste, smell, and look.

I once spent a week in Australia with David Hoffman, historian of fast food and author of the definitive text *The Joy of Pigging Out*. The subject so preoccupied David that he once changed apartments to be nearer a tiny west Los Angeles café called the Apple Pan, which served superlative burgers and apple pie.

During his Australian visit, he sampled numerous dishes but seldom more than a mouthful of any one. In the whole vast continent, only one taste caught his attention: Peppermint Crisp, a chocolate-coated green mint candy bar that, like Proust's madeleine, revived memories of a childhood treat. "I'm taking back a bagful," he told me. "Just simple mint honeycomb dipped in chocolate, but I love them. The true essence of good food is that it brings back the taste of childhood. And these are just like the mint candies my mother used to dole out on special occasions."

I'd been in France ten years before I met another of these gifted individuals, and it took a further five to become . . . well, I won't say "friendly with": a better expression would be "tolerated by." But at least we were on sufficiently good terms to share the occasional meal, and for me to provide an audience as he delivered his jaded commentary on the decline of food not only in France but around the world.

I'll call him "Boris" because he reminds me of Boris Lermontov, the ballet impresario in the film *The Red Shoes*. He even looks a little like Anton Walbrook, the suave Austrian who plays Lermontov. Both are pale, as if they shun sunlight. Both have thick, dark mustaches and full heads of hair, in each case a little too long. Their pouchy, skeptical eyes mirror a dry humor just this side of bitterness.

Anton Walbrook

Boris and I were first thrown together at one of those fund-raising banquets for a worthy expatriate cause. Had either of us been paying, we would not have attended. I'd been invited as the Token Writer. As for Boris . . . well, who knew? He may have known something incriminating about the event's organizer. It was equally possible he'd seen the well-dressed crowd outside and simply strolled in.

Dinner was the cliché salmon with dill sauce, broccoli and new potatoes, all in boil-in-the-bag portions from some industrial restaurant supplier. Everyone got the same thing.

Everyone, that is, but Boris. He got an empty plate.

Was this an insult, to emphasize that he hadn't paid? In that case, my plate should have been empty, too.

Whatever the reason, he made no comment, just picked up his knife and fork and started to eat an imaginary meal.

The imitation was perfect. He cut and chewed non-existent salmon, took sips of invisible wine, mopped up illusory sauce with a phantom scrap of bread. Once, he even asked a neighbor to pass the salt. The people on either side simply didn't notice the empty plate or, if they did notice, just didn't believe their eyes.

As everyone finished, he, too, put down his knife and fork and for the first time met my eyes across the table.

Leaning forward, he murmured, "Diet."

I might have forgotten all about Boris if I hadn't, by chance, run into him again a few weeks later. A friend who knew the more obscure byways of literary Paris had once taken me to a little restaurant tucked away in the maze of streets in the tenth arrondissement around the Gare de l'Est. It's called La Chandelle Verte—The Green Candle. In other respects ordinary, it's a place of pilgrimage for admirers of Alfred Jarry, author of the absurdist classics *Ubu* and *Ubu Roi*. (Ubu's preferred expletive was *"De par ma chandelle verte!"*—By my green candle!) Jarry memorabilia decorates the walls, and the café frequently figures in events staged by those hard-core Jarryists, the College of Pataphysics.

Boris was studying a portable chess set. There was no sign of a plate.

Wondering if he would remember, I asked, "Still on that diet?"

It took him a second to recognize me. When he did, he just nodded to the opposite chair. I sat down.

"Who's winning?"

His game hadn't progressed far. In fact, not a single piece had moved.

"Too soon to tell."

As the waiter approached, Boris said, without looking up, "He'll have the cabbage soup."

We sat in silence till the soup arrived. To cook a good cabbage soup is a challenge. I expected the conventional gray sludge with the consistency of wallpaper paste. This was different. Potatoes had gone into it, cubed, with the skins still on. White beans, garlic, and onion enlivened a robust stock. There was cabbage, of course, but not too much. The cook had peeled off the tough outer leaves and used only the heart, which ran through the broth in crunchy shreds. The combination was delicious.

By the time I was mopping up the last drops of the

soup, the chess game had advanced. A white and a black pawn faced each other on K4.

"Do you recommend a dessert?" I asked.

"The *Gâteau Normand au Calvados* isn't bad."

I looked at the menu. "I don't see it."

"Oh, they don't do it here. But they make a good one at the Café Croissant."

Feeling the ground slipping away ever so slightly beneath my feet, I asked, "In the second? Where Jean Juarès was assassinated?"

He looked up. Was there a little respect in his expression? I probably imagined it.

"That's one distinction of the place, I suppose," he said. "Personally, I go there for the gâteau. They bake on Thursdays."

Taking this for an invitation, I turned up the following Thursday just before lunch. In 1914, a fanatic with the theatrically appropriate name of Raoul Villain shot socialist politician Jean Juarès here. In those days, the Café Croissant had special police permission to stay open all night for the benefit of journalists who had to keep late hours. Juarès and his friends were celebrating having stopped the government from introducing a compulsory three-year military service. Villain, a right-wing militarist, leaned through a window from the street and killed Jaurès with a single shot. A wall plaque commemorates the fact, and Boris was sitting below it. This time he wasn't playing chess with himself but doing a crossword puzzle. Or at least thinking about it, since, though he held a sharpened pencil, he hadn't filled in a single square. I couldn't read a word of the paper. It appeared to be in Cyrillic.

The plate in front of him held a slice of moist-looking cake.

"That will be the *Gâteau Normand au Calvados*?" I asked as I reached for the menu.

"Don't bother," he said. "This was the last piece." He pushed his plate toward me. "I saved it for you."

It was moist, crusted with coarse sugar, wedges of apple baked in, the whole thing fragrant with apple brandy.

As I ate, he studied the crossword. "'Vampiric member of the family Petromyzontid,'" he said. "Seven letters."

"Lamprey?"

"I believe you're right. Thank you." But he didn't write it down.

There is a book to be written about my assignations with Boris, always at cafés that had a claim on immortality or notoriety. Usually some writer had worked there, or an artist had made it his favorite subject. Occasionally a building of historical importance, since demolished, once occupied the site.

Visitors to Paris assume cafés are places to drink coffee and perhaps to eat, but to Parisians that's only a small part of their significance. Herbert Lottman, who analyzed Parisian expatriate life more acutely than almost anyone else, knew their importance.

> *One could not only meet friends in a café but conduct business there, spend half a day writing letters, or even a book. One needed no invitation to strike up a conversation with a stranger at a neighboring table, and an appointment in a café often replaced an invitation home. It kept home inviolate, and if home was a garret, all the more reason.*

A traditional café of the 1890s. The waiter carries the day's newspaper, provided free to clients but attached to a wooden rod to prevent stealing.

Boris never invited me to his home. For all I knew, it could be a seventh-floor *chambre de bonne* in the funky nineteenth arrondissement or a *maison particulière* in snobbish Neuilly. If he had a family, he never spoke of them. In the same way, even though we met in dozens of cafés, I almost never saw him eat, except, occasionally, a slice of *pain Poilâne*, the wholemeal sourdough bread that was one of the few modern products for which he had any respect.

As well as being chapels to his love of food, restaurants were also classrooms. Boris would order *poulet chasseur* on my behalf, then, with surgical skill, dissect a joint to demonstrate the elasticity of the tendons that showed this to be not some pathetic battery bird but an authentic *poulet de Bresse* that had been allowed to eat and reach maturity in the open air.

A spoonful of mashed potato sparked a dissertation on the cooking and preparation of the purée that Marcel Proust fed to the musicians of the Poulet String Quartet when he summoned them to his apartment at 2:00 a.m. to play César Franck and stir his memories. It came from the kitchens of the Ritz Hotel, directed by the great Escoffier.

Boris was so eloquent on the subject that I looked up the recipe, *Pommes de Terre à la Crème*, in Escoffier's

Le Guide Culinaire. It specifies Vitelotte or new kidney potatoes. They must be boiled in their skins, peeled immediately—a miserable chore for some *sous-chef*—then sliced and put into a pan with boiling cream. When the potatoes are soft and the cream reduced, the mixture is whipped with a hand whisk and "finished" with yet more cream. No wonder the musicians wiped their plates.

Boris could speak of food with the passion of a lover. But like the old man on the back steps in my film, he'd eat no more than a spoonful. Was he like those tasters of wine, tea, or coffee who need only a tiny amount to gauge quality? Or did he rather resemble Casanova in old age, having enjoyed so many beautiful women that perfection bored him, and he could be aroused only by the ugly and grotesque? Either way, Boris lived in the same belief that food wasn't about appetite but appreciation. In every respect, he qualified for the term used by UNESCO to define a person who maintained the quality of food for its own sake. Fine shades of meaning separate the terms for connoisseurs of food. A *gourmet* enjoys food and eats well, but not to excess. A *gourmand* loves food so much that he gorges himself; he's a glutton. But a *gastronome* is someone for whom the study of food and the maintenance of its excellence means infinitely more than the satisfaction of mere appetite. He doesn't so much enjoy or love food as revere it—and one does not eat what one reveres.

In *The Red Shoes*, Lermontov declines to watch Vicky Page dance at a musical evening thrown by her mother. Ballet, he tells her, is his religion. "And one doesn't really care to see one's religion practiced"—he makes a contemptuous gesture that encompasses the gaudy décor and chattering guests—"in an atmosphere such as this." Boris the gastronome was no different. To celebrate food in a public restaurant would have been, to him, like munching a hot dog in church. And I mean a hot dog with *everything*.

I hesitated for a few weeks before I told Boris about my project. We were in the courtyard of the Grande Mosquée de Paris. He drank mint tea, which I never liked, while I nibbled on one of those nut cookies called *ma'amoul*. I felt like Burton on his secret pilgrimage to Mecca, an unbeliever enjoying the pleasures of Islam.

I explained what I had in mind.

"I don't like your chances of finding anyone to roast an ox."

"I only want to see if these dishes still exist. It isn't a real dinner. It's a dinner of the mind. I thought you'd approve."

"You've had worse ideas," he conceded.

"You'll help me out, then? Advise me?"

"As long as I don't have to eat any of these things."

"No risk. I promise. So . . . where would you begin?"

"As it says, a meal begins with an apéritif."

"But which one?"

"What about your friend Karl?" he said. "I'd ask him."

Karl was another expatriate writer and a famous drinker. But . . . Boris and Karl acquainted? I didn't know that. Though now I came to think of it, they'd both been at that dinner where Boris ate his invisible meal. Was there a covert association of such men, meeting in out-of-the-way cafés for the same ambiguous exchanges that passed between Boris and me? Was I just one cog in a vast conspiracy? Paranoid fantasies ran through my head. There was that feeling again, of things slipping out of control.

Four

First Catch Your Tipple

"By the way, this café we are nearing is reputed to have the worst anisette in Paris. Shall we try it?"
We did, and it was unspeakable.

S. J. PERELMAN, *The Saucier's Apprentice*

All over the world, waiters automatically ask if you want a drink before your meal, something to sharpen the appetite: an *apéritif*—from the Latin *aperitīvus*, "to open." But only in France is that question pregnant with social significance.

The French believe there are some things one doesn't drink before eating. But they don't tell you what these might be. As a rule, no drink menu is offered until the wine list appears. Clients are expected to express their preference in aperitifs without guidance and, in doing so, to reveal their knowledge and experience or lack of it.

Coffee and tea, for instance, are never drunk at the beginning of a meal, only at its end. Beer, juice, and sodas are for the beach, not the dinner table. On the other hand, if you order a whiskey or martini, you risk being pigeonholed as an alcoholic. And to request "just a glass of water" is almost the worst choice of all, since it's seen as evading the question. Naturally, water will be provided. But what do you want to *drink*?

Ian Fleming, preoccupied, as always, with lifestyle, included some advice in *For Your Eyes Only*.

James Bond had his first drink of the evening at Fouquet's. It was not a solid drink. One cannot drink seriously in French cafés. Out of doors on a pavement in the sun is no place for vodka or whisky or gin. No, in cafés you have to drink the least offensive of the musical comedy drinks that go with them, and Bond always had the same thing—an Americano—Bitter Campari, Cinzano, a large slice of lemon peel and soda. For the soda he always specified Perrier, for in his opinion expensive soda water was the cheapest way to improve a poor drink.

Being Australian puts me in an awkward position when it comes to choosing an *apéritif*, since, unlike countries as diverse as Patagonia and Finland, Australia had no distinctive national tipple. Gullet-numbing iced lager

satisfies 99 percent of the population, leaving a fragile but discriminating fraction to enjoy the country's excellent wines. When I was a boy, wine was drunk only in gloomy and sinister wooden-floored bars called "wine lodges," where shabby men and women sipped the day away on sweet sherry and port. It wasn't until German and Austrian winemakers emigrated in the 1940s that we learned how to make wine and to appreciate it.

One lone attempt at an ethnic Aussie brew dates back to World War II. Troops stranded in the green hell of New Guinea invented Jungle Juice. A pumpkin was hollowed out and the cavity filled with dried fruit, sugar, and water. The pumpkin was then hung from a tree to ferment. As the rind rotted through, a murky fluid leaked out. The amount of alcohol varied, as did the flavor. I once asked a veteran what it tasted like.

"We didn't give a fuck about the taste," he said curtly. "Only the effect."

Boris was right to suggest Karl as an authority on alcohol, since he'd made its appreciation his life's work. His capacity was titanic. To accept an invitation for a drink at his apartment above Place de Châtelet was to invite oblivion. One of his mojitos turned my legs to rubber, and his martinis were so close to pure gin I suspected he followed the legendary advice of just bending over the glass and whispering, "Vermouth."

But the Karl who opened the door the day I arrived to see him was barely recognizable. Where was the portly personage I'd helped down the stairs after our last party? He'd lost at least fifty pounds, and his trousers, showing just a suspicion of flare, suggested he'd resuscitated clothes that had been hanging in his closet since the seventies.

"What happened to you?"

He had the grace to look embarrassed. "I went on the wagon, dear boy. It was my liver," he explained as he led me into his living room. "My doctor said it belonged in the *Guinness Book of World Records*."

I'd barely sat down before he went on. "But I haven't offered you a drink. No reason why you should give it up just because I have."

"No, please," I said. "This is a scholarly visit."

But abruptly there was a glass in my hand: the stemmed tapered tulip, customarily reserved for sherry, that the English call a schooner and the Spanish a *copita*. This one didn't contain sherry, but something the color of weak tea. I sipped and gasped.

"What the hell is this?"

"Maple syrup schnapps. A friend in Toronto brews it himself. I've never tried it, but I was curious." He looked at my glass, a little wistfully. "What's it like?"

"Well, as the Germans say, 'also works in your cigarette lighter.'"

"Yes, I fancied it might be a bit robust. But drink up, my dear chap. And tell me about this scholarly query."

As I explained my project, I braced myself for the onslaught. Karl was one of those people who, if you inquire, "How much is two and two?," is likely to reply, "Now, that's a very interesting question. Take the Assyrians . . ."

As expected, the request for suggestions of obscure but tasty aperitifs opened the floodgates.

"Well, you would need to begin with the Italians. The French imported the habit from Italy in the nineteenth century. Italians love their home brews. Wormwood, caraway, anise . . . If you can soak it in wine with a bit of sugar, and the result doesn't send you blind, you've got an aperitif."

He had a thought. "Or you can use alcohol instead of wine In that case, they call it rosolio." His eyes went nostalgic again. "Not a bad drop, rosolio."

I had less happy memories. Once, at the end of a dinner in Florence, our hostess announced that two other guests, a plump couple from the alpine north, had brought some homemade liqueur. The bottle, tall and conical, its exterior molded in a relief of fronds, flowers, and fruit, was a masterpiece, complementing the lustrous golden liquor swirling inside. Reverently, a servant decanted a few spoonsful into enameled thimbles of glass, fragile as eggshells.

"*La signora e il signore,*" explained our hostess, who refused a glass, I noticed, "own the world's largest plantations of"—she didn't need to finish; I could smell it— "licorice," she concluded.

I took a sip anyway. The nectar of the gods tasted like cough medicine.

"No, not rosolio," I said, "if you don't mind."

"Very well. Leaving aside Italy for a moment, let's concentrate on France. Well, I hate to say it, but the obvious choice is Kir."

He was right. Kir, a flute of white wine sweetened with a shot of fruit syrup, usually *crème de cassis*, made from blackcurrants, had insinuated itself into the drink menus of the world, and in a surprisingly short time. Though it sounds like it should have been around for centuries, it doesn't appear in any book of cocktail recipes until the 1950s.

Félix Kir was a priest, a leader in the anti-Nazi Resistance, mayor of Dijon from 1945 to his death in 1968, and a pioneer in "twinning" towns. Thanks to him, Dijon was linked with Cluj in Romania, Dallas in the United States, Mainz in Germany, Bialystock and Opole in Poland, Pécs in Hungary, Reggio Emilia in Italy, Skopje in Macedonia, Volgograd in Soviet Russia, and York in Great Britain. Scarcely a week went by without a deputation from one of them paying a visit. Facing yet another reception, Kir saw he could encourage both local winemakers and the bottlers of *crème de cassis* if he mixed their products in a single drink.

Kir comes close to being the perfect aperitif. It's alcoholic, but only mildly. It has an element of the soft drink, but the wine adds a touch of sophistication. Best of all for the French, the many different styles of Kir provide an opportunity for the individual to display discrimination, knowledge, or intelligence—in other words, to show off.

For a start, it's considered chic to ask for *Kir royal*, made with champagne rather than still wine. Even more obscurely, you can request *Kir cardinal*, which uses red wine, not white. But to see a waiter really baffled, demand a *Kir communard*. It's the same as a *cardinal* but is named in honor of the anarchists of the Commune who briefly controlled Paris in 1871 and were, as you can explain to your impressed friends, Reds.

Then there's the syrup. Traditionally, it's cassis. But you can request *Kir framboise*, with raspberry liqueur, or *Kir pêche*, which produces a pretty golden drink—though, like most things made with peach, it is a trifle insipid. My favorite was invented by Florian, a boutique maker of jams and candies with a tiny factory wedged into a canyon next to a roaring stream below the Provençal town of Vence. Want to see a wine waiter lost for words? Ask for a *Kir royal aux pétales de rose Florian*. The barman hasn't heard of it? Then, of course, you can explain how it's made, which will make you the focus of attention among not only your dinner companions but the entire restaurant.*

When you ask what syrups are available, the waiter will nominate three or four, but almost never *mure*—blackberry. Edith Wharton spelled out the reason in her little book *French Ways and Their Meaning*, published in 1919.

---

* For anyone who harbors such low intentions, the recipe (among others) is included at the back of this book.

Take care! Don't eat blackberries! Don't you know
they'll give you the fever? Throughout the length
and breadth of France, the most fruit-loving and
fruit-cultivating of countries, the same queer
conviction prevails, and year after year the great
natural crop of blackberries, nowhere better and
more abundant, is abandoned to birds and insects
because in some remote and perhaps prehistoric past
an ancient Gaul once decreed that "blackberries
give the fever."

Aside from this obscure passage, I've never found a single reference to this prejudice. But it's undeniable that, across the Channel, blackberries are gathered wild, made into jams, and baked into tarts. Yet they hardly ever appear in French markets. And nobody wants to serve a blackberry Kir.

Why? Perhaps because 1919 was the year of the influenza pandemic that killed between twenty and forty million people—the "fever" everyone so rightly feared. Before they learned the infection was worldwide, people in France blamed the recently ended war—specifically noxious vapors from the polluted battlefields and the buried dead. Such vapors would naturally rise in a warm, damp, misty month such as October, which is

also the time when blackberries sometimes develop a toxic mold called *Botryotinia*. In that atmosphere, a few cases of blackberry poisoning, or even rumors of them, would have been enough. And after almost a century, some vestige of the belief persists.

I like Kir," I said to Karl, "but it's a bit . . ."

"Middle class? Know just what you mean, my boy. Next thing, they'll be selling it at McDonald's. But what about pineau? I'd have thought it would be your first choice, your wife being from Charente."

He was right. Pineau, made with juice from the first pressing of the grapes, mixed with cognac, is a favorite in the region where Marie-Dominique's family originated. It's drunk at almost every formal meal—a good reason to avoid it for my imaginary banquet.

"I was hoping for something more adventurous."

As expected, Karl took this as a challenge. "Adventure? Well, if you want adventure . . ."

Throwing open his drink cabinet, he revealed four shelves with bottles at least five deep. If Ali Baba had been an alcoholic, this would have been his treasure cave.

"What about pastis, Picon, sambuca, arak, or even the real stuff: absinthe?"

"I don't like anise."

"But, my boy, you haven't tasted this." He flourished a bottle with a garish label in Spanish. "Anis Najar, made only in Arequipa, Peru. Forty-six percent alcohol—same as vodka. Or this . . ." He hauled out another bottle. "Chinchón. *Seventy percent* alcohol. With this, I wonder the Spanish haven't put a man on Mars." More bottles. "Mustn't forget Scandinavia. Aquavit? Lovely stuff. Swedish schnapps." He held up a murky flagon with a handwritten label. "This is Finnish. *Lapin Eukon Lemmenjuom.* Translates literally as . . . um, 'Lappish Hag's Love Potion,' apparently. Brewed from blueberries. Not sure where I got it, but has to be powerful. You know the Finns. Born with hollow legs."

• • •

A n hour later, stepping out, unsteadily, into boule- vard de Sébastapol, I had to clutch the doorframe as the floodlit Tour St.-Jacques reeled against the night sky.

I'd meant to ask Karl how he knew Boris. But such mundane questions dissolved in the haze of alcohol. My banquet was well and truly launched. Karl had con- vinced me that to give my guests anything but the mild- est of aperitifs was to invite disaster and place them in the state in which I had found myself. They could all have classic Kir, and lump it. All I needed now was something to feed them. And, of course, an ox.

Five

First Catch Your Sturgeon

On the other side of my plate was a smaller plate, on which
was heaped a blackish substance which I did not then know
to be caviare. I was ignorant of what was to be done with it
but firmly determined not to let it enter my mouth.
Marcel Proust, *À La Recherche du Temps Perdu*

At the start of a love affair, the bed becomes a raft of
pleasure, adrift on an ocean of expectations. Midnight discoveries and drowsy revelations at dawn are the
common currencies of discourse.

At such a time, in the depths of our first passion,
Marie-Dominique murmured, "I have a secret."

Could there be yet more to discover from this sorcer-
ess to whom I was so completely in thrall?

"Tell me."

She wriggled closer. "I will whisper it."

She brought her mouth close to my ear. "I love . . ."

I held my breath. What erotic revelation hovered on those delicious lips?

"No, I adore . . ."

Yes? Yes?

". . . caviar."

I grew up with no concept of caviar, except as a symbol of luxury and excess. Before arriving in Europe, I'd not only never tasted it. I hadn't even seen it. This was hardly surprising, coming from a country where any food not recognizably derived from a sheep, cow, pig, or chicken was regarded as Satan's work.

If any had been offered, I might have reacted like Tom Hanks in the film *Big*. A twelve-year-old boy in the body of a man, he retains his juvenile prejudices against new flavors. At his first taste of caviar, he spits it out in disgust. But, then, Proust didn't like it, either. Some pleasures are not simply wasted on the young but incomprehensible to them. Can anyone enjoy caviar who does not also relish cunnilingus?

As puberty invades the body, so do new appetites. Bitter, salt, and spicy no longer repel. Olives, oysters, and anchovies, wine and whiskey, reveal their attractions. The first experience of alcohol is a male rite of passage, since it marks the moment at which you no longer want to spit it out. In theory, the stronger the brew, the more firmly it cements your maturity. Americans favor whiskey, "that bitter liquor that only men drink," though I tend to Samuel Johnson's opinion that "claret is the liquor for boys, port for men, but he who aspires to be a hero must drink brandy." In Australia, we just got beer. In that, one sees one of the many essential differences between my native country and the wider world of drinking.

Returning (from London) to France not long after I moved there, I ate a quick lunch at the seafood bar in London's Heathrow airport. A refrigerated cabinet behind the counter was stacked with small, flat cans. I remembered my new wife's murmured confession.

"Tell me about the caviar," I said to the waitress.

Her manner changed. No longer just a man enjoying a smoked salmon sandwich and a glass of chardonnay, I displayed Aspirations.

On the counter she placed three cans, as seductively colored as poker chips: sky blue, orange red, and deep oceanic green.

"Beluga, Osetra, and Sevruga," she said.

With the help of pictures in a brochure, she explained the three types: pea-size Beluga, golden Sevruga, and small, gray Osetra.

"They come in four ounces and twelve ounces."

"How much for the four ounces of Sevruga?"

I've forgotten what I paid, but in 1990 Beluga sold for thirty-two dollars an ounce in New York, Osetra was thirteen dollars, and Sevruga, ten dollars, so my four ounces of Sevruga probably cost about forty dollars. At the time, it seemed a lot. The waitress obviously thought so, too, since the caviar came with a warm smile and, more practically, a Styrofoam traveling pack with dry ice inside to keep it cold. You never got that kind of attention with baked beans.

As a coming-home gift, the little can could not have been more successful.

"Caviar!" Marie-Dominique hugged me. "It's so long since I had any!"

"We can eat it tonight."

"Oh, we can't have it *tonight*."

"Why not? I'm curious to know what it tastes like."

"You don't understand," she said, placing it into the fridge. "Let's save it for the weekend."

By Saturday, it was already apparent that dinner would be an Event. The table was set with candlesticks, the best Limoges china, linen napkins rather than paper, and a wine cooler. As a final touch, Marie-Dominique had unearthed an ancient spoon from the depths of the china cupboard.

"It belonged to my great-grandfather."

The spoon's bowl was molded of some beige organic substance.

"What's it made of?"

"Deerhorn. You never serve caviar with metal."

That evening, the lights of the dining room were dimmed, the candles lit. The tiny can nestled in ice beside a bowl of crème fraîche and a metal dish with something wrapped in a napkin. I peeked. Fat bite-size pancakes, blinis, warm from the oven. Almost the last thing brought to the table was a bottle of vodka, straight from the freezer and coated so thick in frost that the label was unreadable. A single green stalk floated in the clear spirit: the herb *Anthoxanthum nitens*, or bison grass.

Cracking the cap of the vodka, Marie-Dominique filled two tiny glasses—more treasures from her grandparents. The spirit was so close to freezing it poured syrup-thick.

"*Nasdrovia*," she said.

We downed the vodka at the same instant. It flooded the mouth with a delicious freshness, followed by a burst of alcohol heat as it trickled down the throat.

Taking a blini, she added a dab of crème fraîche, then scooped some caviar with the horn spoon. So did I. At the same instant, we popped the morsels in our mouths. On palates cleansed by the vodka, the tiny eggs ruptured—multiple explosions of delight.

Aaaaah! *Now* I understood.

This, then, is the secret of caviar. It's not good because it costs a lot; it costs a lot because it's good. When Edward Fitzgerald mused in his *Rubaiyat of Omar Khayyam*, "I often wonder what the Vintners buy / One half so precious as the Goods they sell," he articulated a thought all of us share on learning that something that gives us pleasure can be had for mere money. Caviar excited just this reaction. Five dollars a teaspoonful? Is that all? I'd have paid double. Triple.

I wasn't alone in experiencing this reaction. News of an embassy reception in New York or Washington will attract a flood of celebrities who attend solely for the caviar. Larry McMurtry describes one such event in his novel *Cadillac Jack*.

> *In three minutes, we were standing next to the velvet ropes, directly in front of the tureen of caviar. I could not get over the avidity of the crowd. Even those who were glassy-eyed from the heat and the crush were trembling with eagerness. Ten seconds later the ropes were removed. It was as if the roof had opened, dropping about five hundred people directly onto a feast. I had no sensation of moving at all, but in an instant Boss and I were at the caviar bowl. I stood directly behind her, functioning like a rear bumper. While people were trying to reach around us, Boss and her peers were eating caviar. One of her peers was Sir Cripps Crisp. "Beastly," Sir Cripps said, while heaping himself another wedge.*

McMurtry doesn't exaggerate. Art critic Robert Hughes sneered about "Warhol and the *Inter/view* crowd at the tub of caviar in the [Iranian] consulate, like pigeons around a birdbath."

Caviar isn't a single product but several. The best is Golden, from the eggs of the Sterlet sturgeon. Once common in Russia and Asia Minor, the Sterlet now survives only on the Caspian coast of Iran. Its caviar almost never reaches the West. When it does, connoisseurs fall on it. In the 1970s, during the rule of the Shah, the certainty of Sterlet at Iranian receptions drew every celebrity in New York or Washington.

Until the 1910s, the best European and American hotels served only Sterlet. But after World War I, supplies dwindled. Any arriving in the United States usually did so by mistake, included in a shipment of the more common Beluga or Sevruga. In 1915, a one-kilo can fell into the hands of Antoine Dadone, who ran Vendôme Table Delicacies on Madison Avenue. He'd just learned from the Russian consul, Mr. Tretiakoff, that, because of the war, all exports of caviar would cease. Dadone sent a pound of Sterlet to Tretiakoff with his compliments. Shortly after, Tretiakoff advised Dadone that the embargo would not apply to Vendôme, whom he promised to keep supplied from his personal stock, shipped in under diplomatic cover.

In 1937, another can of Sterlet arrived at Vendôme, in a consignment of Beluga from Astrakhan. Beluga was selling for fifteen dollars a pound; add two zeros for today's prices. For the Sterlet, Dadone asked a preposterous fifty dollars—two months' rent on the average house.

"Who would pay such a sum?" demanded a journalist. Dadone shrugged. "Who buys diamonds at Cartier?"

A British officer, after capturing a Nazi headquarters during World War II, found a refrigerator filled with cans of caviar. Deciding that his men deserved a taste of this luxury, he gave one to the mess sergeant. The man returned almost immediately. "Excuse me, sir," he said, "but this blackberry jam tastes of fish."

Stories like this bolster the fear in some people that they won't "get" caviar, that it requires a cultivated palate. We say of something too good for the public that it would be offering "caviar to the general." In fact, an appreciation of caviar is independent of class or character. The first time Louis XV of France tasted it, he spat it out. Yet in the 1980s, tiny snack stalls scattered around Moscow's Red Square offered only two things: a sugary ice cream and a slice of rye bread topped with a heaped spoonful of caviar. Both cost the same—in those days, about twenty-five cents—and sold equally well. And you would never suspect from her poetry that Sylvia Plath, while working at *Mademoiselle* magazine in her student days, haunted buffets at press lunches, gorging on caviar. "Under cover of the clinking of water goblets and silverware and bone china," she wrote in her autobiographical novel *The Bell Jar*, "I paved my plate with chicken slices. Then I covered the chicken slices with caviar thickly as if I were spreading peanut butter on a piece of bread. Then I picked up the chicken slices in my fingers one by one, rolled them so the caviar wouldn't ooze off and ate them."

Marie-Dominique and I were enjoying caviar in the twilight of availability. The female sturgeon can't be "milked" like the salmon. She must die before her eggs can be extracted, washed, sieved, and packed, sometimes lightly salted, into cans.

I was haunted by a scrap of film showing Russian fishermen netting a giant sturgeon. Thrashing sluggishly in the muddy water, she looked clumsy and unthreatening, dumbly unaware of the precious few kilos in her belly, for which she would shortly be slaughtered. What if, for every kilo of butter, a cow had to die? Would we enjoy our *croissant au beurre* or buttered toast quite so much? On the evidence of the sturgeon and caviar, it appears we would relish it all the more.

In the 1990s, the Soviet Union and Iran both gave belated thought to the dwindling sturgeon population and severely limited caviar sales overseas. In 2005, the United States banned Caspian caviar altogether. From 450 tons a year, Russia's exports fell to 87 tons in 2007, all from non-Caspian fisheries, and Iran's to 45 tons from a 1997 peak of 105 tons. Prices in the West soared to £9,000 a kilo—about 15,000.

We can gauge caviar's growing rarity from the way it's packaged. Until the 1890s, it was shipped in wooden casks holding three or four kilos, similar to those used for oysters. As supplies dwindled and prices rose, the packers moved to porcelain jars of about half that volume. In the early twentieth century, these gave way to one-kilo cylindrical cans, with a wide rubber band to keep the unpasteurized contents airtight. Today, although French producers still use these, the trickle of Russian caviar reaching the West does so in smaller batches. "On a grey Brussels morning to the Marché Matinale," described a 2005 British newspaper report, "clandestine traders sell smuggled, wild caviar from the boots of their cars for the bargain price of €50 to €80 per 100g can."

To fill the vacuum, all sorts of products annexed the name. The purée of eggplant known for centuries around the Mediterranean as *baba ghanoush* was renamed *caviar d'aubergine*, and a salsa with black beans and black-eyed peas became "Texas caviar." Tapioca, the starch of the cassava root, usually sold in pearl form, was touted as "vegetable caviar."

In supermarkets, jars of red and black fish eggs promised the delights of sturgeon caviar at a fraction of the price. They came from the lumpfish, otherwise known as the sea toad. One look at this morose bottom-feeder was enough to convince anyone that it could never produce anything so subtle as caviar. Skeptics put lumpfish eggs in a strainer and ran cold water over them. The black or red dye sluiced out, and with it all flavor. The remaining eggs, tiny and transparent, tasted of nothing at all.

A New York restaurant startled everyone by offering caviar with ice cream and chocolate syrup. The "Golden Opulence Sundae" came in a crystal goblet with an 18-carat-gold spoon. The dish included five scoops of ice cream made from the world's most expensive ingredients, wrapped in sheets of edible gold leaf, and topped with a dish of Grand Passion caviar, a form of what was described as "American Golden dessert caviar," sweetened and infused with passion fruit, orange, and Armagnac. The Golden Opulence sold for $1,000, which made it, for a while, the world's most expensive dessert.

Mixing caviar with fruit sounded like the worst waste since Jermaine Jackson, brother of Michael, while staying in a Swiss hotel, doused a bowl of Beluga with ketchup. However, a little research unmasked American Golden Dessert caviar as something much less precious. It came from the whitefish, a cousin of the salmon, common in the Great Lakes. Retailing at eighteen dollars an ounce, whitefish eggs are fat and pink, like those of the salmon, and share the look, though not the taste, of Sterlet. Once you wash off the mucus-like goo that coats them, they're as bland as the roe of the sea toad.

At one time, caviar was as common a component of a great meal as foie gras. Escoffier served it liberally, always Golden Sterlet. What a coup if I could somehow find any kind of caviar for my dinner, however imaginary.

The week I started my quest to create the perfect banquet, Boris had chosen to hang out at Café au Chai de l'Abbaye, on rue Buci. He was in a booth at the back, and reading, or affecting to read—he took no interest in recent news—a copy of *Le Monde*. While he was reading, I peered more closely at the headlines:

PRESIDENT DE GAULLE
ANNOUNCES REFERENDUM

795 arrests, and 456 injured in overnight rioting.

The paper was dated May 24, 1968.

I glanced around the café. "Did the *soixante-huitards* meet here?"

It wasn't impossible. The Chai has a long political tradition. During the 1930s, it was a favorite with the émigrés who lived in rented rooms along rue Jacob. Many were on the run from informers and assassins sent by Franco, Stalin, or the secret police of half a dozen Balkan monarchies. A big mirror on the rear wall reflects the whole café and the sidewalk outside. If you sit in the rear booth, with your back to the door, you can see everyone in the mirror, but unless you move your head slightly, to show your reflection, you're invisible. Boris obviously knew this, since he had chosen just this spot in which to sit.

"I heard this story . . ." I began.

"I hate stories."

Ignoring him, I went on: "A Russian princess in the 1920s is driving through Charente—"

"Oh, the fisherman and the sturgeon."

"Yes. What do you think?"

"Probably true."

"Really? We're talking about the same one? A Russian princess just happens to be driving across a river in France when a fisherman hooks a sturgeon—?"

"—and to her horror, he rips out the insides, including the caviar, and throws them away. You doubt it?"

"Well, it's a bit coincidental."

"The unlikely is almost always true. Nobody has taken the trouble to make it plausible. It's the obvious you need to worry about. Anyway, I'm told they even kept the princess's parasol. It's in the local museum."

"But . . . sturgeon in France?"

"There are sturgeon all over the world, or used to be. I expect the river was the Gironde. Lots of sturgeon there. And Russians settled in that region after the revolution—those that got out with any money. It reminded them of the Black Sea."

"And French sturgeon really produced caviar?"

"Why not? French and Russian cows both make

milk. Why shouldn't French and Russian sturgeon make caviar?"

"Then why isn't it sold?"

"What makes you think it isn't?"

"Have you ever tasted it?"

"Of course. So have you, probably. When French growers first started producing, all the snob restaurateurs turned up their noses. So they routed their product through a cannery in Odessa. Once it had Cyrillic on the lid, the *grosses têtes* couldn't get enough."

L ater that summer, Marie-Dominique and I went in search of French caviar along the lazy rivers of Charente.

Even with directions, the fishery took some finding—probably by intention. For more than an hour, we cruised narrow country lanes where two cars could barely pass and the trees arched over the road, a tunnel of green that protected us from the worst of the southern sun. The voice on the GPS unit seldom let up. *In two hundred meters, turn left, then right. At the roundabout, take the second exit . . .*

Our route dwindled down to a rutted dirt lane running parallel to a narrow river—the Isle, which flowed eventually into the Dordogne. After a kilometer, it petered out in a potholed dirt parking lot. A big nineteenth-century house filled the space between us and the river. Opposite was a more recent and nondescript two-story brick building. Only a small printed sign on its front door, "No Caviar for Sale," told us we'd arrived.

B oris was right. French caviar did exist, but only just. By the time the French realized the commercial potential of sturgeon, the Gironde was the sole river that still had a population. Growers imported Russian sturgeon and bred them with the local fish. Now there were fisheries scattered around southwest France and northern Spain, producing about fifty tons of caviar a year.

"There's not a lot going on at the moment," said the manager as he showed us around the building. "It isn't the season. They grow through the summer, and we harvest between October and April."

Occasionally, women passed us, dressed like lab technicians in white coats and plastic hair caps. They regarded us without warmth. Freeloaders must be an occupational hazard.

"You'll want to see them," said the manager, and led us out into the sun.

The ponds, more than twenty, each as shallow as a children's wading pool, filled the space between the road and the river. The bottoms of most were painted blue or white, though a few were black, making it hard to see the sturgeon that swam sinuously, dark-backed and velvety.

I reached down toward the cool water, then pulled my hand back.

"They don't bite," said the manager. "No teeth. They're bottom-feeders. Not like salmon. More like sharks. No real skeletons. Their bones are . . ." He made a flexing motion with his hands, as if bending an invisible rubber hose back and forth. Never use words when a gesture will do.

We walked between the ponds in the hot sun, sweating, longing to join the sturgeon in the cool water that gushed, purified, from the river just beyond the trees. Their numbers were uncountable: scores in each pond, the size of big salmon, gliding and slithering. Young men patrolled, scooping pellets from large bins and scattering them across the water.

Facts flowed from the manager like water from the river. These fish were young, these older; these were males, so of no use except for their meat (very tasty; marinated in yogurt, then barbecued—some Russian visitors had cooked it for him). These were females, though two years away from producing a worthwhile quantity of eggs. And one pond held Sterlet, imported from Siberia as an experiment. If they thrived, the company might soon be selling the Golden caviar currently hogged by commissars and imams.

"Do you like caviar yourself?" I asked.

He looked incredulous. "Of course."

"How do you eat it? With vodka and blinis?"

"No. Dry champagne and a little black pepper."

I recognized the hunger in his tone. We faced each other like two men over the table at a buffet supper, united only by appetite. It wasn't death that was the Great Leveler but Food.

"And how much do you produce?"

"Altogether? In a good year? About six tons."

All these creatures, sacrificed for just six tons. I thought of the female sturgeon in the scrap of film, struggling in the Caspian mud. Hundreds of thousands of lives snuffed out for the 450 tons once eaten in a single year. How to weigh that against our delight as we relished Beluga in the Paris candlelight? Or did it add to the savor that each pearl was a tiny death?

I would like to say it put me off caviar for life. But within twenty-four hours, I was lifting a spoon heaped with Beluga, ready to see if it really tasted better with black pepper and champagne than with vodka.

Somewhere in my notes was the fishery's price list. They sell their best caviar for €1,614.60 a kilo: roughly $2,000. Four ounces is 113 grams, so my can from 1990 would now cost me about $130—about $20 for each teaspoonful.

Was there any better appetizer than caviar with which to begin my imaginary banquet?

I couldn't think of one.

Was it worth the fortune it would cost?

I engulfed the delicious mouthful.

Yes.

Definitely yes.

Six

First Catch Your Madeleine

Let them eat cake!
  Attributed, erroneously, to Marie-Antoinette

Within a few weeks of vowing to create the ideal banquet, using the "lost" dishes of France, the sheer size of the task dawned on me.

Leaving aside the major problem of finding an ox and the people to both roast and eat it, I needed to choose the number, variety, and style of the other dishes, the wine and other accompaniments, and—this being a French banquet—the underlying philosophy of the meal. I feared that, in an appropriately culinary metaphor, I had bitten off more than I could chew.

On the principle that, to untangle a can of worms, one begins with a single worm, I began with a part of the meal I knew I could handle. As my guests sipped their Kir, one should them offer an *amuse guele*—a nibble. And what could be better than a petit four—a little cake? I even knew which cake it should be—a madeleine.

As my father was a pastry cook, the aroma of fresh-baked cake permeated my childhood. I grew up around dark, moist fruitcake; cupcakes topped with frosting and colored sprinkles; and bouncy sponges, split and sandwiched back together with whipped cream and strawberry jam.

In particular, I remember his towering wedding cakes, battleships of the baker's art, triple- and occasionally quadruple-decked, armored in marble-white marzipan. Swags of royal icing draped every side. I can see my father's sure hand painstakingly looping sugary strands from cones of parchment paper, pinning the end of each swoop with a tiny silver sphere called a cachou.

I assumed, when I moved to Paris, that, in this capital of patisserie, cakes would be even more popular. Not so. While the French enjoy fruit tarts and pastries, they view cake with skepticism. The standard item of *patisserie* has a creamy filling, enclosed in a stiff pastry case. Or it could be a tart, filled either with the sticky lemon sauce that I grew up calling "lemon curd," or with pieces of fruit thickly glazed with sugar syrup and firmly bedded in *crème patisserie*, a thick custard that keeps the fruit in place. Individual pastries enclose soft mousse in *choux* pastry or seal it firmly under a chocolate shell.

Cake, when it appears, is rigorously segregated. In supermarkets, fruitcake is packaged as *cake Anglaise*—cake English style. Sponge is unknown, and pound cake exists only as *quatre quatre*—four by four—made with equal quantities of flour, sugar, eggs, and butter. For weddings, most couples opt for a *pièce montée*, a tall cone of profiteroles (bubbles of cream-filled pastry lacquered with a caramel or chocolate glaze). We had one for our own wedding.

Why don't the French like cake? Mainly it's the crumbs. In Regency England, the worst social disaster that could befall a snuff-sniffing man of fashion was to drip brown snot onto his snowy white cravat. Imagine, then, the embarrassment of a French courtesan who, glancing down, finds her lover, while browsing her décolletage, sporting a mustache flecked with reminders of afternoon tea.

To solve this problem, the French developed their own versions of cake: dense, moist, chewy, and, above all, crumb-free. Among French tea-time nibbles, the most popular are the *financier*, the *macaron*, the *cannelé*, and the madeleine. The *cannelé*—pluglike, rubbery, dark brown—is grooved down the sides: *cannelé* means

"channeled." The oblong *financier* is named for its resemblance to a gold bar. The *macaron* looks like a miniature hamburger, its halves joined by a layer of confiture.
Most elegant of all, the plump, round madeleine is baked
in a mold that gives it the fluted shape of a scallop shell.

The baba, soaked in syrup or rum, might drip but will
never crumble. Nor is there much risk of fallout from the
beignet, a twist of deep-fried dough, the ancestor of the
doughnut. The *cannelé* contains double amounts of sugar
and eggs, plus a dousing of rum. As for the madeleine, *financier*, and *macaron*, part of the flour is replaced by ground
almonds. In each case, the result is the same: no crumbs.

And if you remark that some French cakes and buns,
in particular the croissant, still crumble, any expert will
explain that it's your fault for not eating them correctly.
If you watch a French person eating a croissant, you will
notice that, before tearing off a morsel, they hold it well
away from their bodies, letting the crumbs fall on the
floor rather than on their clothes.

After that . . . well, I'll let the American journalist
Robert Forrest Wilson explain:

> *The croissant is of a crisp, flaky texture, and if
> one attempts to eat it dry, it explodes into flying
> fragments at every bite. It is, however, not eaten*

dry—it is dipped into coffee. It is not only good form in Paris to dip one's croissant but practically necessary. It is a bun specialized for dipping.

Since 1924, when that was written, the croissant has undergone even further refinement in the interest of avoiding crumbs. The fashionable choice in breakfast breads these days is a croissant filled with a paste of . . . yes, that's right: almonds.

I once tried to persuade my father to widen his horizons by baking some madeleines for the shop. He was busy making Lamingtons, an Australian favorite, beloved of pastry cooks, as they use up stale pound cake. Cut into blocks, the cake is dunked in chocolate syrup and then rolled in desiccated coconut.

"What's a madeleine?" he said. "I've never heard of them."

"Here's the recipe." I showed him the passage laboriously translated from the *Larousse Gastronomique*.

He wiped his hands on his apron and took the slip of paper but read only as far as the ingredients.

"Ground almonds! You know what they cost? You want me to go broke?"

After I moved to Paris, I made a point of sampling every kind of French pastry. Some took a little more

A Nun's Fart

effort than others. Maybe it was my Catholic upbringing, but I always felt furtive biting into the caramel-frosted cream-filled puff known as the *pette de nonne*—nun's fart.

But I was soon converted to the moist, lemony *financier*; and as for *macarons*, vividly colored, and flavored with lemon, raspberry, chocolate, caramel, or passion fruit, I had to agree with the cook who wrote, *"Ils sont irrésistibles, avec leur petite coque craquante et leur intérieur fondant"*—"They are irresistible, with their little crunchy shell and their melting interior."

Above all, I remained steadfast in my devotion to the madeleine, though not solely for culinary reasons. How many cakes could be said to have inspired a literary masterpiece?

L ate in the summer, I asked Louise, "Would you like to take a trip to Illiers?"

"Of course. Love to."

A year earlier, such a question would have earned a glare and a muttered "I'm busy." But whatever demon seizes children at fifteen, transforming them overnight into sullen monsters, had just as suddenly relinquished her, leaving behind a sunny and bright young woman.

She even crawled out of bed at 7:00 a.m. for the two-hour train trip. We were early enough at Gare Montparnasse to snatch some coffee in a deserted café and share a blueberry muffin, fending off a trio of bold sparrows—*piafs* in French slang—that scavenged crumbs right off the table. In tribute to their size and fearlessness, Edith Gassion, a small and feisty street singer of the 1930s, with a poignantly piercing voice, rechristened herself Edith Piaf—although her choice was ironic: sparrows can't sing.

An hour later, our TGV was gliding across the plains of La Beauce—the Bread Basket. The Beauce is Kansas with a French accent. A few weeks before, we'd have looked out on amber waves of grain. Now the fields were stubble, their wheat stored in the silos that, as in Kansas, loomed next to every station. Over the landscape lay the lassitude that follows the harvest. Slowing into towns, we glimpsed empty streets, shuttered houses, shops with blinds drawn, and dogs drowsing under chestnut trees.

Switching on my Kindle tablet, I clicked to the text downloaded the night before: *Du côté de Chez Swann* (*Swann's Way*), the first volume of Proust's *À la Recherche du Temps Perdu*.

"*Longtemps, je me suis couché de bonne heure . . .*"— "For a long time, I used to go to bed early . . ."

I first read those lines as a teenager, in the stifling heat of an Australian country town, hunched over the book on a verandah with the *rush rush* of cicadas in my ears and the fronds of a pepper tree rattling on the tin roof.

> *Sometimes, when I had put out my candle, my eyes*
> *would close so quickly that I had not even time to*
> *say "I'm going to sleep." And half an hour later the*
> *thought that it was time to go to sleep would awaken*
> *me; I would try to put away the book which, I*
> *imagined, was still in my hands, and to blow out*
> *the light; I had been thinking all the time, while I*

was asleep, of what I had just been reading, but my
thoughts had run into a channel of their own, until
I myself seemed actually to have become the subject
of my book.

I knew that feeling! Drowsing over a book, I'd wake with a start, thinking I was still reading—then realize I'd invented that next part in my sleep, the writer in me taking over like an automatic pilot in an aircraft.

I held out the Kindle to Louise. "I downloaded *Du Côté de Chez Swann*, if you want to read about Illiers."

"It's all right," she said. "We did it at school." Making a pillow of her coat, she folded her arms and closed her eyes. "Wake me when we get there."

At Chartres, we transferred to a two-carriage train with cars hardly larger than those of the Paris Metro. Three girls boarded at the last minute, hauling bicycles. Otherwise, we were the only passengers. And once we left the station, the rusted rails running along-side showed that only a single line was in use. We were truly leaving civilization behind.

I kept browsing through *Du Côté de Chez Swann*, losing myself in its long, unwinding sentences.

The French, initially, didn't get Proust. One editor grumbled, "I just don't understand why a man should take thirty pages to describe how he rolls about in bed before he goes to sleep." Publishers doubted anyone could recall every detail of events that took place thirty years ago and scoffed even more when Proust explained the prosaic event that unlocked this ability: the taste of tea into which he'd dunked a few crumbs from a madeleine.

I skimmed through the text to that passage.

And suddenly the memory returns. The taste was that of the little crumb of madeleine which on Sunday mornings at Combray (because on those mornings I did not go out before church-time), when I went to say good day to her in her bedroom, my aunt Léonie used to give me, dipping it first in her own cup of real or of lime-flower tea.

Was it my childhood as a baker's son that made this image so poignant? I looked at Louise, drowsing opposite. Already an accomplished cook, she was particularly skillful with pastry and cakes. Maybe there really were things that "ran in the family."

•　　•　　•

Two hours after leaving Paris, our little train sub-
sided to an exhausted halt at Illiers. We climbed
out into the sun. There wasn't even a platform—just
a stretch of asphalt and the unmanned station. Across
the tracks, beyond a field of weeds, some derelict brick
buildings slumped, apparently held up by the vines that
wreathed them. The flat crack of a shotgun carried
across the fields: hunters out for rabbits in the stubble.
Otherwise, there was no sound at all.

We walked through the deserted station into the
sunny square in front.

In 1971, the locals thought enough of Proust to
rename the town Illiers/Combray, incorporating his
fictional name for the community, but after that, their
enthusiasm waned. A statue might have been asking
too much, but they could at least have erected a sign:
"Hometown of Marcel Proust."

Instead, the square was dominated by an obelisk com-
memorating the dead of the 1914–18 war. Perched on the
top, a bronze rooster, the *coq Gallois*, symbolized France's
cocky fighting spirit. It was a silent statement of relative
values. Literature was all very well, it told us, but national
pride, what the French called *la gloire* (glory) came first.

Heavy chains attached to empty shell casings fenced
off the memorial. On one of these, facing the monument,

perched the only living thing in sight, a gray pigeon. It didn't fly off as we approached. Rather, it appeared to be in rapt contemplation of the rooster on top of the obelisk.

"Maybe it lost someone," Louise said. "One of those pigeons that carried messages."

A single tree-lined avenue out of the square suggested a route into town, so we took it. When I looked back, the pigeon still hadn't moved.

Thirty minutes later, at a table on the deserted central square, Louise sipped an *eau à la menthe* and I drank a beer. We had seemed to be the only strangers in town until an English family colonized the next table. After ordering a single coffee, mother, father, and both children disappeared, one after the other, into the dark interior.

"That toilet must be the most popular spot in town," I said.

"At least it's *open*."

Illiers certainly presented no threat to Disneyland. Everything except the café and the church was shut. This included the sparse one-room visitors' center, where a stony-faced lady handed us a map, and the former home of Proust's great-aunt, now a museum. We'd arrived there at midday, to be told by the lone *gardienne* that it was about to close for lunch.

"When do you reopen?"

"Two thirty," she said, with a look that suggested I'd asked a silly question.

Two and a half hours for lunch? This was so excessive that I recognized the statement of principles behind it. This Marcel Proust was only a *writer*, people! Nobody really *important*. Opposite, a bakery advertised itself as "where Tante Léonie bought her madeleines." It, too, was closed, with blinds pulled down and no suggestion they would ever rise again.

"To live in Combray," Proust wrote, "was a trifle depressing." I could see why. As Luke Skywalker complains of his home planet in *Star Wars*, "If there is a bright center to the universe, this is the place furthest from it."

For two hours, we explored anyway. Illiers had been modestly prosperous once, but those days were gone. Shutters had been up for decades at the *bains-douches municipaux*, where, in the days before home plumbing, one could take a weekly bath. Nor were there any women at the public laundry where wives and housekeepers once knelt around the communal pond, gossiping as they pounded their clothes clean.

At 2:30 sharp, the *gardienne* at the house of Tante Léonie, more cheerful after her lunch, unlocked its black metal gates.

The little house had barely changed since Proust lived here between the ages of six and nine, at the end of the 1870s. In the kitchen, simple country pots and pans covered the table. Climbing the narrow, winding wooden stairs, we dipped our heads to pass through low doors, smiled at the narrow beds, the flowered wallpaper, the faded oil paintings—all just as Proust describes. Only the attic was different. It now contained a photo gallery of Marcel's family and friends, a menagerie of bushy beards, extravagant hats, and men in stiff collars glaring at the camera. If you smiled in those days of long exposures, it tended to come out as a ghastly grin.

Finally, we stepped into Léonie's bedroom. On the table next to her bed, in a glass case, like holy relics, sat a white ceramic teapot; a cup, saucer, and spoon; a dish of dried lime leaves; a bottle of Vichy-Célestins mineral water; and a delicately fluted madeleine.

As I stood in reverent contemplation, Louise pointed to the mineral water.

"Vichy-Célestins. The kind *mamine* likes."

She was right. Her grandmother—my mother-in-law, Claudine—shared an older person's preference for fizzy mineral water. And both slept in almost identical beds, in the Second Empire style, with the same scroll-backed wooden headboards.

It surprised me how serious an interest Louise took in the house. Confident I knew everything of importance about Proust, I'd refused the sheaf of documentation offered by the *gardienne*, but she'd accepted one. She referred to it as we walked around, quoting what Proust wrote about the wallpaper, a painting, the orangerie, no bigger than one of the bedrooms, at the bottom of the small garden. Louise had grown up with Proust and "done" him at school. As part of her *patrimoine*— her cultural heritage—he was worthy of respect, like Balzac, Zola, Gide.

My appreciation was different. I was a fan. For me, the visit was sacramental, akin to taking the waters at Lourdes. It was enough for me to sniff the air, smell the dust, stand in the little garden and look up at the windows through which he'd gazed a century and a half ago. *He had been here.*

In Proust's kitchen

Louise

The monument at Illiers, with pigeon

Just as we stepped out onto the street again, the blind in the window of the patisserie rattled up and a girl turned the sign on the door from "*Fermé*" to "*Ouvert.*"

They sold madeleines—not as Tante Léonie had bought them but prepacked in polythene. We bought half a dozen bags—gifts for the family, souvenirs. I waited until we got on the train before I opened one and took a nibble. If I expected the same revelation as Proust, I was disappointed. Not bad but a bit dry. And, I suspected, made with plain flour, with no powdered almonds. Maybe with some lime-flower tea . . .

I held out the bag to Louise, curled up again with her coat, half asleep.

"Want one?"

She opened one eye. "No, thanks. I'm on a diet."

She started to nod off again, then thought of something.

"By the way, did you know it wasn't originally a madeleine he dipped in the tea?"

"Not a madeleine? Of course it was a madeleine!" I reached for my Kindle and proof.

"In the book, he *made* it a madeleine," she said, "but in *Contre Saint-Beuve* he describes what really happened."

She shuffled the papers given her at the house and read out a passage from Proust's earlier book, regarded as a dry run for his masterpiece.

The other night, when I came in, frozen from the snow, and not having got warm again, since I was writing by lamplight in my bedroom, my old cook suggested making me a cup of tea, which I never drink. And by chance, she brought with it some slices of pain grillé. I dipped the pain grillé into the cup of tea, and the moment I put it in my mouth I had the sensation of smelling geraniums, orange blossom, and a sensation of extraordinary light, of happiness.

"*Pain grillé*? Proust's madeleine was . . . a piece of toast?"

"Apparently." She saw my disappointment. "The idea's the same."

"Yes. I suppose so."

But a small light had just gone out. Once again, Proust was proved right. Nothing lasted. Though time could be briefly retrieved in memory, it inevitably passed. And if the instant of insight can change one's life, another instant can change it back.

At the end of *Du côté de chez Swann*, the narrator tries to retrieve memories of Swann and his wife by returning to the streets where they once lived. But though the buildings and the people look more or less the same, time has changed both them and the older Proust who observes them.

> *The reality that I had known no longer existed. It*
> *sufficed that Mme. Swann did not appear, in the*
> *same attire and at the same moment, for the whole*
> *avenue to be altered. The places that we have known*
> *belong now only to the little world of space on which*
> *we map them for our own convenience. None of them*
> *was ever more than a thin slice, held between the*
> *contiguous impressions that composed our life at*
> *that time; remembrance of a particular form is but*
> *regret for a particular moment, and houses, roads,*
> *avenues are as fugitive, alas, as the years.*

Oh, well—as Marie-Antoinette might have said, "Let them eat toast."

Seven

First Catch Your Fungus

The waitress said, "We have a wonderful sandwich of grilled Portabellas with Asiago on country bread dressed with extra virgin olive oil and served with a julienne of jicama and blood orange."

"What's a portabella?," Shirley said to me.

"A big mushroom," I said.

She looked at the waitress and frowned. "A mushroom sandwich?"

From *Chance* by Robert B. Parker

I n all my agonizing over the ingredients of my banquet, one emerged as essential. No great dinner could be complete without the unique taste of truffle.

Between 2004 and 2005, I spent a lot of time in Italy, hired by an American company to create the plots, character outlines, general background, and, in time, write some of the screenplay for a TV drama series about that great fourteenth-century outpouring of creativity known as the Renaissance. Though the project was doomed from the start, it was an exhilarating if troubling task. To visit men and women descended from the families that employed Leonardo and Raphael, to handle actual letters written by Lorenzo de' Medici, to stroll after closing time through the empty galleries of the Pitti Palace, alone with the work of Botticelli and Tiepolo, was worth more than any salary I was paid— when it *was* paid, that is.

I never got used to the modern-day aristocrats who often neither knew of nor cared about their heritage nor preserved it. One couple brought in an expensively bound family history published years before but obviously never opened—except, they discovered to their embarrassment, by their children, who'd used some blank pages to scribble in crayon. Another duke demanded testily, "Why do people make such a fuss about this Machiavelli fellow? He was just a secretary to one of my ancestors."

Occasionally, good taste and intelligence prevailed. As we left one palazzo, our hostess paused by a glass cabinet filled with tiny figurines and *objets d'art*.

"A few of our family treasures," she said (as if her entire house didn't deserve that description). She opened the door of the case and lifted out a fragile object.

"As you enjoy cooking, John, you might find this interesting."

I recognized a mandoline. Chefs use them to slice vegetables or cheese. A panel of wood or plastic is supported at a forty-five-degree angle on metal struts. As you slide something down the panel, a raised blade cuts uniform slices that fall through a slot to a plate below.

Most mandolines are solid and robust—they need to be—but this one was so tiny it could sit on her open palm. A delicate filigree of metal supported a slide made of some pale, yellowing material that wasn't wood.

"Silver," she said, "and ivory. Early nineteenth century."

"Is it a toy?" asked our producer. "For a doll's house?"

Meeting my eye, the contessa turned down one corner of her mouth. *How can you work with such people?*

"No," I said, answering for her. "I believe it's for truffles."

Few people hold up their end of a cocktail party conversation when the subject turns to fungi. The moment I ask if they prefer French girolles to the larger but, in my opinion, less tasty Romanian variety, they glimpse friends on the other side of the room whom they just *must* talk to.

A Scots traveler named John Lauder, who visited France in 1665, was disgusted by the very idea of eating mushrooms. "It astonished me that the French find them so delicious. They gather them at night in the most sordid and damp places. They cook them in a terrine with butter, vinegar, salt and spices. If you have them grilled, you can imagine you are biting into the tenderest meat. But I was so biased that I couldn't eat them."

For years, I agreed. My region of Australia knew only one variety. Large, flat, gray-white on top and pink underneath, they appeared after rain in paddocks where animals had manured the ground. Without being precious about it, I hesitated to throw a lip over anything that could trace its ancestry so directly to cow shit.

If that hadn't prejudiced me, the standard cooking method would have. Everyone fried them, sliced, in butter. This caused the juices to ooze out in a liquid the color of boiled newsprint. Canned mushrooms looked exactly the same, right down to the monochrome slime, flatteringly described as "butter sauce." This convinced cooks of my parents' generation that they'd hit on the perfect recipe. Raised on canned food, they believed that the factory-made project represented the yardstick of perfection. The greatest achievement of a cook was to create something indistinguishable from the same product as canned by Crosse and Blackwell or packaged by Sara Lee. "It's as good as a bought one," they said in satisfaction, delighted that their mushy, overcooked spaghetti looked just like the product as canned by Heinz. Traditionally, stewed mushrooms were served with steak. As the horrid gray mixture was ladled on, it mixed in a particularly unpleasant way with the meat juice. This topped my list of culinary Bad Sights until my first encounter with carpetbag steak. For this Aussie favorite, a pocket was cut in a double-thick slice of rump and filled with raw oysters. As you sliced the meat, the oysters dribbled out. I had to wait for the film *Alien* to see anything quite that nasty.

Britain proved no better than Australia at exploring the possibilities of fungi. Though mushrooms flourished in their fields and forests, the British shared John Lauder's suspicion about anything gathered in damp and sordid places. They solved the problem by creating the button mushroom. Smooth, white, and rubbery, the button is factory farmed—and, unfortunately, near tasteless. But at least you know where it's been.

Buttons also exist in France, where they're called, in a snub to the British and others, *champignons de Paris*. Every French kitchen has a few small cans, stored next to similar cans of corn niblets. Add a can of corn and one of mushrooms to a bag of lettuce hearts, toss in a few strips of ham and gruyere, and you have a dinner salad. Mix them with eggs for a quiche. Good on pasta, good on pizza, good in chicken stew. One size fits all.

I much preferred the "wood mushrooms" that appeared in the market for a few weeks each August. Fluted golden girolles; black *trompettes de mort*; the small and pallid *pied bleu*, dead white except for the slightly sinister blue tinge at the foot of the stem; pale, chewy pleurotes, aka oyster mushrooms; and tastiest of all, the fragrant, meaty porcini, or *cèpes*—all shared an air of wildness. Misshapen, speckled with dirt and straw, and even, in the case of *cèpes*, showing signs of nibbling by insects, these uncouth country cousins seemed to mock the well-bred buttons. In letting them into the house, you took your safety in your own hands. No wonder the Spanish called them *la burla de la naturaleza*—nature's bad joke.

Few mushrooms have a strong flavor. On holiday in the Dordogne, after a day foraging in the woods, I ran our finds past the local pharmacist. After examining each one, he placed three to one side.

"So these are poisonous," I said, cautiously poking one of the three.

"No," said the pharmacist. "*These* are the edible ones."

"Then these"—I indicated the brimming basket—"are all toxic?"

"No, they're harmless. You *could* eat them. They just don't taste of anything."

This is true of most fungi. The art of cooking them is to maximize what little flavor they have. My best mushroom recipe came about by accident. Trying to duplicate a *ragoût forestier* we'd eaten in a country restaurant, I fried some girolles and *cèpes* in butter with salt, pepper, and crushed garlic.

Initially, the result was disappointing. As the juices ran together, it formed the same gluey sauce I hated in Australian mushrooms. Fortunately, a phone call distracted me. I turned down the heat to answer it. When I returned, most of the liquid had boiled away, allowing the butter absorbed by the mushrooms to run back out into the pan, leaving the mushrooms coated with a savory glaze that concentrated their forest flavors. A handful of chopped parsley and some fresh black pepper turned the dish into a perfect accompaniment for grilled meat. It was also delicious folded into an omelette, while the same recipe using girolles alone gave flavor and contrast to steamed or grilled fish.

I might have remained constant to the rough fellowship of *champignons forestiers* had it not been for my trips to Italy for the TV series.

In Florence, the production manager and his assistant met me off the overnight train. At 10:00 a.m., it was too late for breakfast, too early for lunch, but, this being Italy, also far too early to start work.

"You like *tartufo*?" the assistant asked.

The only "tartufo" I knew was a frozen dessert, a ball of vanilla ice cream encrusted with chocolate sprinkles. Did the Italians really eat ice cream for morning tea? Well, when in Rome (or at least Florence), do as the Romans do.

"Of course," I lied.

But Procacci, the shop on via de Tornabuoni to which they took me, was no ice-cream parlor. All varnished wood, terrazzo floor, and display cases of curved glass, it hovered between café and upmarket cake shop. As we sat down at a tiny table, the production assistant brought us a plate of bite-size buns.

"*Panini tartufati*," she said.

So *tartufo* was Italian for "truffle." That chocolate-coated ice cream had been a clumsy attempt to duplicate the look of a *truffe noire*.

I bit into the soft white bread, spread with butter creamed with white truffles, and was instantly seduced. When Marie-Dominique joined me on the project, Procacci became our favorite Florentine hangout. On the night train back to Paris, we habitually took the same picnic supper—a dozen of its *panini tartufati*, with a bottle of champagne. The meal always ended with mild dissatisfaction. Next time, we told ourselves, we'd buy an extra half-dozen, and really gorge. We were converts to the creed of Colette: "If I can't have too many truffles," she said, "I don't want any at all."

Even the best chefs use truffles sparingly, mostly because of their price. Black or white, they sell for around $100 an ounce. The cost reflects the fact that, unlike most mushrooms, they can't be cultivated. They grow wild, and only around the roots of oaks—a tree less common in France than Britain. Lately, some French cultivators have tried "farming" truffles, planting an oak grove, fertilizing the roots with spores, and waiting a year in the hope of a crop. For the time being, however, most trufflers hunt them with animals.

Our feeble sense of smell can't detect them underground, but badgers, boars, certain dogs, and a particular kind of fly have no such problem. Hunters train dogs to scent the truffle and hope to get there before the hound has rooted it out and wolfed it down for itself. Some tried to train pigs to do the same job, but after a few fingers were lost tussling with voracious porkers, dogs became more popular.

For a few weeks one autumn, the most expensive fruit and vegetable seller in the Marché Saint-Germain displayed a sealed jar next to the cash register. Inside, resting on rice, to absorb the moisture, sat three black truffles.

"How much?" I asked, trying not to salivate.

"Three hundred and fifty euros a kilo," said the owner. I decided to sleep on it.

By chance, the following weekend took us into Périgord, not far from Carpentras, France's truffle capital. In a small town, we browsed the weekly produce market, thinly supplied as the last green vegetables and summer fruits disappeared in the autumn chill.

In Australian country towns, the railway station or town hall often carries prominently the date 1888. Building something new in the year of Queen Victoria's Golden Jubilee, her fiftieth year on the throne, had been a way of Australians reminding themselves they were really still British.

But my maternal grandparents were Swedish and German, so my cultural roots were partly in continental Europe, not Britain. In coming to Europe, I felt for the first time that not only the people but the landscape and buildings were speaking "my" language. Over the cultural abyss between Australia and the rest of the world, I sensed an invisible bridge linking me to the knowledge Europeans acquire at birth.

Still a stranger, even after twenty years in France, I walked that bridge gingerly, trying not to look down into the depths of my ignorance. It was easier in the countryside, in villages, and particularly in churches. A compact chapel of the Middle Ages, set on a headland above the Atlantic, with a vineyard on one side and a graveyard on the other, offered more evidence of my place in the world than the most elaborate cathedral of red sandstone baking in the Australian sun.

For the first time, I felt an affinity with not only the Catholicism in which I was raised but the earlier faiths on which it rested: the rituals of earth magic, of sacrifice and divination that, oddly, resonated at times with those of the Australian aboriginals. The gods never move as far away from one another as we move away from them.

All this crossed my mind in that market. The last seller in line offered the least stock. His table was small and almost bare: just an ancient brass scale, with tiny iron weights, and a few flat metal dishes. Why did he appear so familiar—alone, dignified, and erect behind his table? Of course. He was the image of a figure from the tarot, *Le Bateleur*—the Magician. Always shown at a table, he displays symbols of three tarot suits—cups, coins, and swords—while holding a rod to signify the fourth, wands, the source of the stage illusionist's magic wand.

Each small dish on his table held a single gnarled black nugget.

Truffles.

I pointed to one the size of a golf ball and asked the price. Solemnly he weighed it on his scale.

"*Seize euros.*"

Sixteen euros? Ridiculously cheap. I reached into my pocket, aware that an ancient tradition was being reaffirmed.

The truffle is the plutonium of vegetation, humming with its own kind of radioactivity. Place a truffle next to butter, in a bottle of oil, or in a bowl of eggs, and its taste invades them all, enriching and perfuming.

My truffle lasted for months. One piece, slivered, went into a bottle of oil, not olive—the fruitiness of which can fight the truffle's flavor—but the less assertive grape-seed. I placed another piece in a crock of unsalted butter, well sealed to stop the flavor from penetrating to every corner of the refrigerator. The rest went into a screw-topped jar with a dozen eggs. Few breakfasts are more delicious than two truffled eggs, soft-boiled, with toast spread with truffled butter.

Truffle and beef is a natural marriage. I copied a dish from La Petite Cour, one of my favorite local eating places. They slice deeply into a *pavé* of rare beef in four places and, just before grilling, place a slice of raw foie gras in each crevice. It's served with tiny boiled potatoes in their skins and a salad dressed with truffle oil. And for a carpaccio that celebrates the pleasures of rare beef, I plunge a piece of filet into boiling oil, leave it there for a minute, then lift it out. The heat seals the meat, leaving the interior almost raw. After the meat had rested for half an hour, I slice it thinly, lay it on roquette (arugula) leaves, sprinkle it with fresh black pepper and *fleur de sel*, garnish with shavings of parmesan, then drizzle with truffle oil.

Cooking with truffles made me even more enthusiastic about their unique qualities, in particular their almost chemical perfume, utterly distinctive, with the power to augment most flavors but not overpower them. After centuries of failing to describe that scent, gourmets stepped back and let scientists try. They came up with surprising, if dismaying, findings.

Apparently, dogs and pigs think truffles smell like semen, which excites them sexually. And dogs locate them, initially, not from the scent of the truffles themselves but from the lingering stink of truffle in their own excrement or that of other dogs, deposited in previous years near those trees where they'd scarfed up the forbidden goodies. The odor is so powerful it can survive sun, rain, snow, and even the canine digestive system.

Someone once called me a "truffle hound" for my skill in ferreting out old books. It doesn't seem quite such a compliment now.

Eight

First Catch Your Lamprey

Hello, suckers!

Texas Guinan

Buying courgette (zucchini) flowers in the market on rue de Seine, I was surprised when the French woman next in line asked how I cooked them. They turn up so seldom in Paris, and for such a short season, that she'd never seen one. But halfway through my explanation—dip them in a tempura batter mixed with grated parmesan, then deep-fry till crisp—she'd lost interest. If I'd said they went straight into a salad, she might have approved, but Japanese batter and Italian cheese? You could almost see her nose wrinkling. *More foreign rubbish. . .*

Given the nation's conservatism about food, how was it, after more than twenty years living in France, that I still hadn't eaten a lamprey? This eel-like fish was once a great delicacy. In the Middle Ages, a pope is said to have paid twenty gold pieces for a fat specimen. Yet, in more than two decades in France, I had never eaten one or seen it on any menu. If any dish was "lost," this was surely it.

And where better to feature such an exotic, richly traditional yet forgotten dish than in my perfect banquet?

"Have you ever eaten lamprey?" I asked Marie-Dominique.

"What is it?"

"A sort of fish. Like an eel."

"Oh, *lamproies*." She grimaced. "No! *Elles sont dégoûtantes!* They live on blood."

It's true—the lamprey is a vampire. Its "mouth" is a cluster of seven serrated suckers with which it attaches itself to a larger fish and drains its juices. A component in its saliva, like that in a vampire bat, prevents its host's blood from coagulating. In Roman times, lampreys were kept in ponds and, according to legend, sometimes fattened on human blood. Supposedly, a slave who broke a valuable plate could be fed to the lampreys. I suspect this tale flatters the fish's sucking ability. All the same, it didn't make one keener to try them out.

Recipes for lampreys turn up often in old cookbooks. In one particularly elaborate medieval method, each "mouth" was plugged with a clove, and the largest with a whole nutmeg—equivalent to roasting a chicken with a whole black truffle in every orifice. The Italians served them with rice in a risotto, and the French in red wine sauce thickened with the lampreys' own blood. King Henry I of England ate so many lampreys during a visit to Normandy in 1135 that he famously died of "a surfeit." A taste for lampreys, albeit "potted" (cooked and preserved in butter), also saw off the poet Alexander Pope.

Lampreys were believed to send women into a sexual frenzy like the one that possessed the mythological nymph Callisto, a handmaiden of Diana, goddess of the hunt. A dish of lampreys made her so hot that Zeus disguised himself as the goddess to lure her into the woods, then, after they'd made love, turned her, in a rather ungentlemanly way, into a bear. Writing in the early 1700s, the British poet John Gay suggested she'd have done better on a vegetarian diet.

> *The shepherdess, who lives on salad,*
> *To cool her youth controls her palate;*
> *Should Dian's maids turn liqu'rish livers,*
> *And of huge lampreys rob the rivers,*
> *Then all beside each glade and visto,*
> *You'd see nymphs lying like Callisto.*

King Henry I liked his lampreys sugared and baked in a crust. When the crust was opened, the syrup, mixed with wine and spices, was ladled onto slices of bread and topped with coin-size slices of lamprey meat.

Fortunately, just as I was about to abandon my search for this elusive creature, I stumbled across a short film on YouTube. It documented how lampreys made a rather desultory attack on some swimmers crossing Lake Champlain, on the Canadian border. I recognized the voice of the film's narrator as an old friend, the Texas-born actor Bill Hootkins. Bill's insinuating bass-baritone made him a favorite for jobs like this and for audio books; his version of the complete *Moby Dick* remains a classic. Though he had small roles in dozens of films, his screen immortality rests on a few moments as the pilot Porkins in *Star Wars*, a fact he found acutely embarrassing.

He regarded his personal best as playing Alfred Hitchcock in the play *Hitchcock Blonde*. Bill was perfect casting, since, like the great director, he loved to eat. In London in the late 1970s, I audited his course on Chinese Cuisine. The "course" consisted of sitting down once a week to a banquet, each time in a different restaurant. To audit, one pulled up an extra chair. Bill spent the evening darting back and forth from the kitchen, noisily supervising each dish in fluent Mandarin.

Sadly, Bill died young, so I never had a chance to ask whether, in his search for new tastes, he'd sampled lampreys. But it was the thought of perhaps outdoing a master that lured me into the quest.

"Assuming I wanted to eat lampreys," I asked Marie-Dominique, "where would I start looking?"

"Nicole might know."

I should have thought of Nicole myself. A doctor in Bordeaux, she and her husband had a farm in nearby Bergerac, where they grew their own produce. An orchard furnished peaches, pears, and miniature green apples, tiny as plums and just as juicy, which we ate straight off the tree, still warm from the sun.

Bordelais cooking is notoriously rich. The first time I visited Nicole, she unsealed a murky liter jar of *cèpes* mushrooms, preserved in duck fat—a gift, she explained, from a grateful patient. On subsequent trips, we enjoyed the contents of similar jars, most of which would have rated a skull and crossbones on any calorie chart.

So I shouldn't have been surprised when, in response to my query, she said, "In fact, one of my patients prepares *lamproies*. Let me see what I can arrange."

•   •   •

A few months later found us driving through the valley of the Dordogne. Vineyards dipped in and out of sight on either side of the narrow, twisting road. For a couple of kilometers, we were stuck behind a cart loaded with gnarled vines, evidently grubbed out at the end of their useful life. I felt we'd slipped back a century, even two. If a man in a red velvet surcoat and plumed hat had leaped his horse across the road in front of us and galloped into the woods, we would scarcely have raised an eyebrow.

On our way, we stopped at the Saturday market in Bergerac. A tall church dominated the square. The stone of its spire had just been cleaned, but they hadn't got around to the side walls, which remained black with age, as if, like the produce sold in their shadow, they had just emerged from the earth.

The farther one penetrates into France, the darker the produce becomes. Along its coasts, food has the glint and shimmer of sun and sea. Even to the landlocked east, on the German border, the Alsatians pickle white cabbage in white wine to make *choucroute*—sauerkraut. But strike inland and the colors deepen and the aromas become more pungent; cheese from Roquefort, prunes from Agen, goose liver from Bordeaux, and black truffles from Périgord.

Almost as common as vineyards around Bergerac are orchards of nut trees. I'd once passed a boozy evening in the courtyard of a nearby château, sampling the owner's homemade digestifs, including an inky variation on the Italian *nocino*, made by macerating walnuts in alcohol. Nobody in Bergerac market offered this funereal tipple, but many had pressed their own oil, which they'd decanted into whatever was handy. We bought golden hazelnut oil in a potbellied bottle that previously held Orangina. As the farmer's wife put our purchases into a plastic bag, she added some scoops of fresh walnut kernels. We nibbled them as we strolled. They were soft, almost juicy; nothing like the parched versions doled out in glassine bags by supermarkets.

After the fruit and vegetables of Paris markets, chosen more for appearance than taste, there was a perverse pleasure in loading up on knobby tomatoes, ripely oozing black figs, and dusty skeins of onions and garlic. No bloodhound was needed to trail us from Bergerac market to Nicole's hilltop farmhouse. Odors of figs, garlic, and hazelnut oil floated in our wake.

Nicole looked over our purchases with resignation. Obviously, we were not the first guests to arrive with more produce than they could possibly eat.

"I thought we'd have the *lamproies* for a starter," she said, "followed by some *brochettes de canard*." From among our purchases, she selected the figs. "These will go with the duck very well."

"Can I see the . . . er . . . ?"

"Certainly."

The liter jar of lampreys looked identical to the one from which I'd eaten *cèpes* years before. The contents were, if anything, even murkier, resembling those organs pickled in formaldehyde and kept in hospital labs to illustrate some particularly loathsome disease.

"She braises them in red wine, with pieces of leek," Nicole explained, "and thickens the sauce with—"

"—the blood. Yes. I remember."

My distaste obviously showed.

"If you'd rather," she said, "we could have something different."

"No, of course not." Appetite didn't come into it. Honor was at stake.

For an hour or two before dinner, we sat under the huge tree that shaded the lawn in front of the house. Nicole passed around a plate of tiny tarts, each with a piece of foie gras and a dab of homemade green tomato chutney. Her husband kept our glasses filled with chilled Monbazillac, for which Bergerac is famous. Why should a sweet, cold white wine such as Monbazillac, Gewurtztraminer, a Botrytis Riesling, or—best of all—Sauternes, marry so perfectly with goose liver? It's just another of those mysteries that make eating in France such a delight.

But when the last drop was drunk, the last tart eaten, and the sun had sunk below the hills, we trooped inside to face the fish that killed a king.

I t was a memorable meal that didn't end until around midnight. With the duck brochettes, Nicole used our figs, quartered and sautéed in butter with spices. Her dessert, even more satisfying, was a variant on tiramisù: a layer of biscuit crumbs, another of fresh berries, topped with a mixture of mascarpone cheese, yogurt, and crème fraîche, beaten with sugar and the grated zest and juice of a lemon.

And the lampreys?

The dark, velvety sauce was so seductive that one quickly forgot blood was its primary constituent. As for the fish itself, its pale pink flesh resembled salmon but with a more delicate texture, closer to sardines. One could see why medieval cooks prepared it with sugar and spice, as the Danes do herring. It needed the lift.

But something for a king to die over? Not really. If I'd been investigating the demise of Henry I, I'd have put some hard questions to the court apothecary.

But as a constituent for my banquet? I thought I could do better.

Nine

First Catch Your King

"A gold service looks very well," said the Countess sadly, "but it allows the food to unfortunately grow cold. I never use mine in my house save when I entertain His Imperial Majesty. As that is the case in most houses, I doubt if His Imperial Majesty ever has a hot meal."

C. S. Forester, *The Commodore*

Back in Paris, I brought Boris up to date on my progress.

He didn't seem impressed.

"So, thus far, you've chosen the aperitif . . ."

"Yes."

" . . . and a madeleine to nibble. Is that it?"

"I found someone who knows how to cook lampreys." I didn't admit that I hadn't liked lamprey meat enough to want it for my feast.

"It's not much, is it?" Boris said.

"It's early days," I protested.

"Not so early as you think. You can't leave things to the last minute. Remember what happened to Vatel."

I left the café in an even more morose state of mind than usual. Boris was right. I needed to plan much more thoroughly if the banquet was to be a success, if only in my own mind. One didn't want to suffer the dreadful fate of poor François Vatel. ...

In St. Paul's Cathedral, London, a circle of black marble set into the floor beneath the center of the dome bears an inscription in Latin.

SUBTUS CONDITUR HUIUS ECCLESIÆ
ET VRBIS CONDITOR CHRISTOPHO-
RUS WREN, QUI VIXIT ANNOS ULTRA
NONAGINTA, NON SIBI SED BONO
PUBLICO. LECTOR SI MONUMEN-
TUM REQUIRIS CIRCUMSPICE Obijt
XXV Feb: An°: MDCCXXIII Æt: XCI.

Or, for those not forced to study Latin in adolescence, "Here in its foundations lies the architect of this church and city, Christopher Wren, who lived beyond ninety years, not for his own profit but for the public good. Reader, if you seek his monument—look around you. Died 25 Feb. 1723, age 91."

"If you seek his monument, look around you" is something most of us would like to have on our graves. To leave the world better than we found it: What greater satisfaction could there be? But occasionally the statement signifies defeat, not success. The Roman orator Tacitus cursed military commanders who boasted of having pacified a region. "They make a desert," he said, "and call it 'peace.'"

It was the fate of one of the most celebrated chefs of the seventeenth century to be remembered for an apparent kitchen disaster and his tragicomic end. I'm reminded of his fate every day, since I live in the middle of it. If you seek the monument to François Vatel, our street would be a good place to start.

Vatel and his son

Fritz Karl Watel was born in Paris in 1631, a poor boy of Swiss parents who Frenchified his name to François Vatel. That's about all we know of his personal life. The few portraits show a proud but melancholy man with dark hair falling in ringlets to his shoulders. His professional credentials are better known. While still in his thirties, he took over household organization for Nicolas Fouquet, financial manager of King Louis XIV, and after that became *contrôleur général de la bouche*—literally, controller-general of the mouth—to one of the most powerful men in France, the Prince de Condé.

Condé, as first cousin to the king and a prince of royal blood, was entitled to be addressed as "Monsieur le Prince" (Mister Prince) but preferred to be known as Le Grand Condé—the Great Condé. In his château at Chantilly, fifty kilometers north of Paris, he lived on a scale lavish even by seventeenth-century standards. One way of keeping score in those days was the number of courtiers you could afford to support. Chantilly housed more than a thousand, all of whom had to be fed. This was Vatel's job, in collaboration with the duke's estate manager and friend, Jean de Gourville.

Half the servants at a palace such as that at Chantilly did nothing but prepare and serve food. Hundreds chopped, ground, minced, and pounded nuts, grains, and spices; picked and peeled vegetables; plucked birds; cleaned fish; and slaughtered, skinned, and butchered animals. Others tended the gardens, orchards, and livestock; maintained the ponds and streams that provided fish; and kept the forest stocked with pheasant, rabbits, hares, and deer, since royalty loved to hunt.

There were numerous pitfalls to cooking for the aristocracy. Royalty believed that some substances were nobler than others, and that the quality of nobility could be absorbed. Renaissance doctors treated the wounds of the rich and mighty with pulverized precious stones. In their last illnesses, Lorenzo de'Medici was dosed with powdered pearls, and Pope Julius II was fed liquefied gold.

This belief extended to food. To be noble, one must consume only that which was also noble, rare, and ethereal. The nobility shunned vegetables that grew in the earth, such as carrots and turnips, and meat from any animal that grazed. Meals were based on fruit, flowers, and creatures that floated or flew, the rarer the better.

They would eat farmyard birds such as chicken or duck in a pinch but preferred those that roamed wild— pheasant, partridge, and quail—or exotic birds such as lark, whose song made them rarer still. Some chefs discarded every part of the lark except the tongue, which they cooked in honey. Swan and peacock also appeared often at royal tables, usually decorated with their own plumage artfully arranged over the roasted bird.

For rarity, however, no bird trumped a tiny member of the bunting family, the ortolan. Hardly bigger than a thumb, they were too small to hunt and had to be caught in special traps. Kept alive until the last minute, they were drowned in Armagnac, plucked, sautéed, and served in individual lidded pots called *cassolettes*, which could hold only one or two birds. One ate them whole, including legs, bones, and intestines (although the more fastidious left the head). Their aroma was so delectable that, before opening the *cassolette*, diners draped napkins over their heads, conserving every whiff.

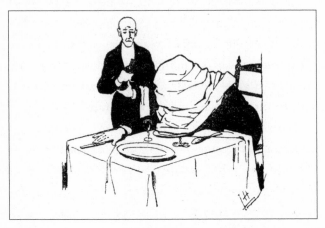

Eating an ortolan

To this day, the mystique of the ortolan survives, even though it's now a protected species. As part of a final banquet, shared with forty friends shortly before his death in 1996, former French president François Mitterand, long ill with cancer, asked for and was served ortolans. The banquet looked back to the days when rarity in what one ate was not only the tastiest sauce but also the best medicine. For Mitterand, in life a figure of almost kingly gravitas and dignity, there was magic in this final feast, each dish an implied appeal for a few more months of existence. One of his guests wrote:

> *He'd eaten oysters and foie gras and capon—all in copious quantities—the succulent, tender, sweet tastes flooding his parched mouth. And then there was the meal's ultimate course: a small, yellow-throated songbird that was illegal to eat. Rare and seductive, the ortolan supposedly represented the French soul. And this old man, this ravenous president, had taken it whole—wings, feet, liver, heart. Swallowed it, bones and all. Consumed it beneath a white cloth so that God Himself couldn't witness the barbaric act.*

•   •   •

S truggling to manage the vast estate of the Prince de Condé, Vatel had no time to cook. Though he's credited with inventing the mixture of whipped cream, sugar, and vanilla known as *crème Chantilly*, this existed before his time. He was more a banquet manager, dealing with tradesmen, arranging the entertainment, fretting over seating plans, keeping enemies apart, making sure discarded mistresses were not placed next to their replacements. He also had to ensure that guests were seated in strict order of precedence, with the noblest closest to the king. This rule persisted into the twentieth century and was overturned only by King Edward VII after the youngest son of a duke was given a better place at his table than Arthur Balfour—a commoner but also prime minister.

W e're used to each guest at a banquet receiving an identical portion of the same dish at the same moment, but until the early nineteenth century this system, known as Russian service, existed only at the court of the czars, who had an unlimited supply of servants. At a czarist banquet, it wasn't unusual for two hundred footmen to serve—one for each guest. Other countries used the less-labor-intensive French service. Diners were presented with successive "avalanches" of food: first a dozen soups, followed by a dozen meat dishes, then a dozen desserts. All the dishes of a "service" arrived at the same time. Guests helped themselves. When they'd had enough, the major-domo signaled "the remove." Servants cleared the table, and another dozen dishes arrived. Anything not eaten was devoured by the kitchen staff or estate workers. The system was conspicuously wasteful, but that was the point. It showed that the host was too rich to care.

Well into the fourteenth century, glasses were too rare and fragile for each guest to have one. A thirsty diner called for a servant, who brought a glass of wine. After he'd drunk, the servant took the glass, rinsed it, and waited for another summons. Nor did diners use flatware. Jean Anouilh in his play *Becket* shows Thomas à Becket introducing his friend King Henry II to a new Italian invention, the fork.

"It's for pronging meat and carrying it to the mouth," Becket explains. "It saves you dirtying your fingers."

"But then you dirty the fork," says the king.

"Yes, but you can wash it."

"You can wash your fingers," says Henry. "I don't see the point."

Initially, forks at table made people nervous. They reminded them of how devils in medieval paintings tormented the damned with pitchforks. A few utensils were provided to transfer food to the plate. After that, everybody used their fingers, which demanded relays of napkins. A typical inventory of a seventeenth-century household lists only eighteen forks but six hundred linen napkins. This aristocratic habit of eating with fingers survives in the French custom of tearing bread rather than cutting it, and using pieces to mop up a sauce.

Author Julian Fellowes spotted a related error in a script for the TV series *Downton Abbey*, set in a British stately home at the time of World War I. "We had a scene in which [Lady] Sybil baked a cake for the first time as a surprise for her mother," recalled the producer. "We shot the cake on the table with plates, forks and napkins. Julian was very upset about this. He said the upper classes would eat with their fingers. He was right." But the reshot scene, though historically authentic, looked so odd to modern eyes that it was never aired.

In 1671, Condé completed a major restoration of Chantilly. To celebrate, he invited the thirty-three-year-old King Louis XIV to inspect and approve the improvements. It was a shrewd move. Though Condé was an important general of the royal armies and a major contributor to the state expenses, Louis still bore a grudge against his cousin for plotting to push him off the throne when he became king at the age of five. Condé hoped the visit might restore to him the king's esteem, since Louis loved to see people grovel. "There was nothing he liked so much as flattery," wrote the Duc de Saint Simon, "or, to put it more plainly, adulation. The coarser and clumsier it was, the more he relished it."

Louis took the bait and sent a courtier to Chantilly to finalize the arrangements for his visit there.

"His majesty doesn't want a fuss," the courtier told Condé. "He just desires some quiet days in the country with a few old and close friends."

But Condé knew the king. "I assume this means his highness will expect food and entertainment of a lavishness to rival the Rome of the caesars."

"Precisely."

"And how many 'old and close friends' may we expect?"

"A mere handful. No more than five or six hundred."

By Louis's standards, this *was* modest. His court at Versailles numbered three thousand people, six hundred of them courtesans, a polite name for mistresses and party girls.

Condé informed Vatel that he would need to cater three consecutive royal banquets, with lavish shows to follow. No feast was complete without a two-hour spectacle of music, dance, theatrical illusions, and fireworks. These were particularly important when entertaining Louis, who fancied himself a dancer. He performed in masques at Versailles and surrounded himself with artists such as the playwright Molière and the composer Lully. It was at Versailles that Lully, beating time with a heavy staff, brought it down on his foot and died of blood poisoning—a rare case of a conductor killed in the line of duty.

The royal visit would cost Condé 50,000 *écus*—well into the millions of modern dollars. However, it was money worth spending if, when Louis left, he'd entrusted Condé with a role in the financial management of France, with all its opportunities for graft.

• • •

L ouis and his retinue arrived on a Thursday, were welcomed by the prince, and shown around the estate. After picnicking in a field of daffodils (planted for the occasion), they mounted up and went in search of game. The hunt continued even after sunset, the king pursuing a stag by moonlight. After this, they returned to the château and sat down to turtle soup, *chicken à la crème*, fried trout, and roast pheasant, followed by a show culminating in fireworks.

But for Vatel, the evening ended in despair. More people than expected turned up to dinner, and there weren't enough pheasants to go round all twenty-five tables. One table complained of getting none and being fobbed off with chicken. Then the weather turned, dampening the fireworks meant to be the climax of the evening.

"My head is spinning," a near-hysterical Vatel told de Gourville. "I haven't slept in twelve nights. And now this terrible thing happens."

Worse was to come. No Catholic ate meat on Friday, so every dish for the second banquet had to be fish or vegetables. The menu probably resembled this one, served to Louis XV in 1757.

First Service. Two soups, one a puree of lentils, the other of shredded lettuce.

Eight hors d'oeuvres: A galantine of sorrel; white beans Breton style; herrings, both fresh and salted, in mustard sauce; grilled mackerel with herb butter; an omelette with croûtons; salt cod in cream sauce; noodles.

Second Service: Four large entrées: Pike Polish style; baked salmon; carp in court bouillon; trout à la Chambord—baked, stuffed and served with a sauce of truffles and oysters.

Four Medium Entrées: Soles with fresh herbs; grilled trout with a sauce of capers and gherkins; perch in Sauce Hollandaise; lotte German style; skate in black butter, and grilled salmon.

Third Service: Eight dishes of baked or fried fish: fried filets of pike; sole and lemon soles; fried lotte; trout, and salmon tails. Four salads.

Fourth Service: Eight hot vegetable dishes: Cauliflower with parmesan; mushrooms baked with anchovies; a vegetable stew; fried artichokes; green beans; cabbage, and spinach.

Four cold dishes: Crayfish, arranged in a pyramid, known as buisson or "bush"; a "Bavar-

*ian cake" or Bavarois, based on a jellied mousse of
fruit; a poupelin, an early version of the Swiss roll,
and brioches.*

The estate could provide pike, trout, and other freshwater fish, but saltwater fish and seafood had to come
from the Atlantic coast, more than a hundred miles
away. At the nearest port, Boulogne-sur-Mer, the previous day's catch had left at dawn, packed in ice and
seaweed, and loaded into four-horse carts, each hauling
3.5 tons. Fresh horses waited every ten miles along the
route. Even then, the trip over unpaved roads and partly
at night would take twenty-four hours.

Descending from his apartments at 4:00 a.m. on
Friday, Vatel had to step over his exhausted staff asleep
along the corridors and in the kitchens. At Chantilly,
a separate building housed senior servants, but valets,
who might be needed at any time, slept in dressing
rooms or closets next to their master's apartment. The
lowliest slept in the corridors, on the floor, the boards
straw-strewn because it was customary to empty chamber pots into the corridor.

At sunrise, an apprentice carried two baskets of fish
into the kitchens—probably the freshwater catch from
the estate's ponds.

Vatel, hysterical with fatigue, demanded, "Is that all?"

When the flustered boy told him nothing else had arrived, Vatel began to rave. De Gourville was sent for and tried to calm him. Even if the fish from Boulogne-sur-Mer had been put on the road at dawn the previous day, it couldn't possibly get there so soon.

But Vatel was beyond reason. "I will not survive this disgrace," he told de Gourville. "My honor and reputation are lost."

Running to his rooms, he wedged the hilt of his sword into the gap between the door and jamb, placed the point against his chest, and thrust himself onto the blade. On the third try, it pierced his heart.

Madame de Sévigné, one of the king's retinue, and a famous tattletale, rushed off a letter to a friend:

Vatel, the great Vatel, Monsieur Fouquet's major domo, who at the moment was serving the Prince of Condé in that capacity, seeing that this morning at eight o'clock the fish had not arrived, and not being able to bear the dishonor by which he thought he was about to be struck—in one word, he stabbed himself. They sent for Monsieur le Prince, who is in utter despair. Monsieur le Duc [de Gourville] burst into tears. You can imagine the disorder which such a terrible accident caused at this fête. And imagine that just as he was dying, the fish arrived. That's all I know at the moment; I think you'll agree that it's enough. I have no doubt but that the confusion was great; it's an annoying thing at a party which cost 50,000 écus.

Most annoying, particularly for poor Vatel. But would anyone kill himself over fish? For many years, the Sévigné letter was the only evidence of Vatel's suicide, and thus a little suspect. Since then, however, other sources have been found to corroborate the story. Explaining them is more difficult. In the film *Vatel*, screenwriter Tom Stoppard offered one theory. Vatel, played by a lumbering Gérard Depardieu, twenty years older than the real Vatel and at least twice his size, is shown romancing one of Louis's courtesans. When he runs on his sword, it's not over fish but in despair at their hopeless love.

Despite Vatel's death, the banquets of Friday and Saturday went ahead and were a great success. As the king and his friends caroused, servants quietly buried Vatel on the estate. Louis apparently knew nothing of Vatel's death until after the dinner. By then, he'd decided to give his cousin another chance.

But this brought "Monsieur le Prince" no enduring good fortune. As Condé had no legitimate children, on his death the title passed to another branch of the family. In the Revolution, mobs destroyed the great château at Chantilly. The Condés had already sold their Paris estates, and in 1790 his townhouse was demolished and the splendid garden cleared to make way for a theater. New streets appeared, including one leading from the Seine to the square in front of the theater. Called rue de l'Odéon, it was the first in Paris to have a sidewalk.

It's also the street on which we live.

On either side, streets called rue de Condé and rue Monsieur le Prince remind us that this was once the property of Le Grand Condé.

But what about Vatel? Well, he, too, has a monument—of sorts.

On rue Lobineau, a few minutes' walk from our front door, stands the tiniest restaurant in Paris. It seats a dozen people only. The menu is simple. So is the wine list. It takes no reservations, accepts no credit cards. It is the very model of the modest Paris eating place. It's called Le Petit Vatel—The Little Vatel.

Ten

First Catch Your Rascasse

Last night we had a bouillabaisse which I couldn't touch because of the terror in its preparation. The secret is to throw live sea creatures into a boiling pot. And we saw a lobster who, while turning red in his death, reached out a claw to snatch and gobble a dying crab. Thus in this hot stew of the near-dead and burning, one expiring fish swallows another expiring fish while the cook sprinkles saffron onto the squirming.

Ned Rorem, *The Paris Diary of Ned Rorem*

Ask any lovers of Italian food about their favourite movie scene, and at least half of them will quote the moment in *The Godfather* when fat Clemenza gives Al Pacino's Michael Corleone his recipe for spaghetti sauce. Some can even repeat it from memory, and in the grating accents of actor Richard Castellano too.

Heh, come over here, kid, learn something. You never know, you might have to cook for twenty guys

someday. You see, you start out with a little bit of
oil. Then you fry some garlic. Then you throw in
some tomatoes, tomato paste, you fry it, ya make
sure it doesn't stick. You get it to a boil. You shove
in all your sausage and your meatballs, heh? . . .
And a little bit o' wine. An' a little bit o' sugar, and
that's my trick.

Some dishes lend themselves to feeding a crowd. Spaghetti with meat sauce is one of them.

Another is bouillabaisse.

Would bouillabaisse suit my banquet? Few fish dishes were as classic, as dramatic, yet as neglected by modern chefs. At the very least, it deserved an audition.

I can remember the moment I began to brood about bouillabaisse.

It was 1970; my first winter in Europe. My companion, Angela, and I had just survived the thirty-day sea voyage from Australia and were living in a village in the east of England. She had become a substitute teacher in the local school system, and I was working on a book.

Looking out through the misted kitchen window of our cottage, across the barren fields, clammy with fog, and listening to the *caw-caw* of crows roosting on the bare branches of the elm trees, all dead of the parasite known as Dutch elm disease, I understood why the collective noun for a gathering of these grim black birds was a *murder*. A flock of sheep. A school of fish. A murder of crows. Yes, it really fitted my mood.

Why had I ever left the sunny south? I needed something to remind me of warmer places. A mango, perhaps, or a papaya. But could either be found within fifty miles? Certainly not in our village shop, where any fruit more exotic than an apple existed only in a can.

Later that week, our luck appeared to change. We were invited to dine with a local painter and his wife.

"I cooked a favorite of ours," said our hostess. "Bouillabaisse."

Bouillabaisse! I'd never eaten it, but the name alone was enough. The most vivid of Mediterranean seafood dishes—shrimp, crab, lobster, in a rich fish stew flavored with tomato and olive oil, colored with saffron, perfumed with garlic, pepper, and laurel. The writer Alfred Capus defined it perfectly: "Bouillabaisse is fish plus sun."

My elation survived until our hostess plunked down a tureen of gray-white soup. Pallid lumps jutted above the surface like torpedoed ships poised over a watery grave. My face betrayed my dismay.

"It's *North Sea* Bouillabaisse, of course," she said. "My mother's recipe, actually. From the war, when you could get only local white fish."

Apparently the Nazis had blocked all imports of garlic, bay leaves, and tomatoes as well, since only leeks and potatoes accompanied the slabs of what I recognized as dogfish, optimistically rechristened "rock salmon." As a treat, I was given the head. Depositing this ghastly object on my plate, the host said jovially, "Good eating there." As it glared up at me, I understood the real meaning of the expression "to give someone the fish eye."

Puttering back home in our unheated Volkswagen Beetle, I asked Angela, "Do you suppose we could manage a holiday sometime?"

"To where?"

I looked out at the dark woods, rimed with frost. "Somewhere warm."

She frowned. "Maybe . . . in the school vacation . . . if someone shared expenses . . ."

Which is how, a couple of months later, our Beetle came bumping down the car ferry ramp at Calais, headed for the Riviera. In the backseat, providing the extra money that made the trip possible, was Cyril.

Cyrils in England are as plentiful as gray squirrels. They may even be the dominant male type. Many, like ours, were teachers. He taught in the same school as Angela and lived in the next village, in a cottage he shared for years with his mother, who had just died. Balding, short, and expressionless, he wore the Cyril Uniform: fisherman's sweater, brown corduroy trousers, suede desert boots. For formal occasions, he added a tweed jacket, elbows leather-reinforced.

Cyril and I distrusted each other on sight. That I was an arrogant Australian and he a snobbish Englishman was reason enough, but he also fancied Angela and couldn't imagine what she saw in me. As Jane Austen wrote in *Pride and Prejudice*, "It is a truth universally acknowledged that a single man in possession of a good fortune must be in want of a wife," and Cyril made no secret of the fact that with his mother gone and the cottage empty, he had marriage in mind. He assessed every eligible woman as a potential partner, but with so little finesse that most reacted like antelopes in a wildlife documentary when they sense a leopard on the prowl. Cyril wasn't discouraged. If anything, rejection made him only more determined.

He kept this up even as we drove across France, but he met his match in Arles. On the Sunday we arrived, local craftspeople had spread their creations on the ground around a small square with a central fountain. Among them, an uncombed but pretty young woman in worn jeans and a tatty sweater sat on a blanket with some pieces of handmade jewelry arranged around her bare feet.

Cyril strolled by, came back for a closer look, then cautiously approached and squatted down, supposedly to examine her trinkets but actually to admire her close-to. As he did so, she met his eyes and, without changing her expression, bared her teeth and growled softly, like a Doberman ready to go for his throat. Cyril recoiled, over-balanced, and sat down hard. After that, a French wife was crossed off his shopping list.

We reached the Mediterranean near the port of Sète, where we'd rented a tiny house in the village of Bouzigues. It was my introduction to La France Profonde—Deep France. Few tourists came here. The locals farmed oysters and mussels and produced a vinegary rosé that telegraphed its unpopularity by being available only in half bottles.

Each morning, at least one housewife walked down our street carrying a large thick casserole dish.

"Cassoulet," Cyril explained when I commented on this. "They take it to the baker while the bread oven is still hot. He lets them leave it there all day. The slow cooking gives the perfect blend of flavors."

Even imparting such harmless information, he managed to suggest I was an idiot. I didn't make it worse by confessing I had no idea what he was talking about, never, as far as I knew anyway, having eaten cassoulet or even seen it.

A split was inevitable. When it came, the cause was food. To save money, we'd agreed to eat at home as much as possible. And since neither Cyril nor Angela liked to cook, the job fell to me. I used fresh local produce, in particular the meaty mussels, which I cooked *marinière*, with white wine. But when I suggested this for dinner one night, Cyril balked.

"Can't we have something else?"

"What's wrong with mussels?"

"I just don't like them."

Nor, it seemed, anything else I cooked.

The dining table became an armed camp, with me preparing the meals for Angela and myself while Cyril made his own. As we explored the local specialties, he stuck to English comfort food: white bread, mashed potatoes, and sausages, with liberal quantities of ketchup.

Angela and I broke into our cash reserves to try cassoulet at the local restaurant. At last I understood what Cyril had explained to me. He was right about the slow cooking. This traditional dish of white haricots with salt pork, Toulouse sausage, and preserved duck—the origin, it's said, of Boston baked beans—needed hours of slow baking to blend its flavors and create the unctuous sauce. It would never taste better to me than on that first encounter.

In the hope of repairing the rift between Cyril and me, Angela brought the three of us together for a final dinner in Sète before we headed back to England. On our last Sunday, we drove into town, following the wide canals along which the fishing boats carried their catch to sell at the quayside.

Despite heavy American bombing during World War II, Sète retained the charm celebrated by its two most famous sons, the poet Paul Valéry and singer-songwriter Georges Brassens. That afternoon, we paid our respects to both.

Valéry is buried in the marine cemetery, a forest of white tombs spreading down a hillside to the Mediterranean. Imagining himself spending eternity in the presence of all this sea and sky, he had felt both subdued and elated.

> *Beautiful sky, true sky, look how I've been changed.*
> *After so much pride, after so much strange*
> *Idleness, now full of strength,*
> *I abandon myself to this brilliant space.*

The graves of Valéry and Brassens could hardly be more different. While Valéry has the ocean, Brassens is buried, as he wished, in the "poor" section, without a view but instead in a grave shaded by pines, and more easily found by those who loved his music. His hopes for the afterlife have a refreshing simplicity. He put one of them into a song.

> *And when, using my grave as a pillow,*
> *A beach girl lies on me, taking a nap*
> *In a swimsuit that's barely there,*
> *I ask Christ in advance for forgiveness*

If the shadow of my cross creeps over her.
For a spot of posthumous bliss.

After our visits, we walked along the stone-edged harbor, where fishing boats docked to unload. I'd never seen so many restaurants in the same place—all, of course, advertising "*le vrai Bouillabaisse.*"

Mediterranean fishermen invented bouillabaisse to use up the spiky, bony, ugly fish left over after the more glamorous stuff had been sold. In Provençal, *bouiabaisso* or *bolhabaissa* means "boil on a low heat,"

Marseilles, the Sailor's Bouillabaisse

emphasizing that the secret of any fish dish is not to cook it too long. The first cooks to develop the dish, sometime in the nineteenth century in the fishing ports along the Mediterranean, had some Italian or Greek blood, They sautéed onions, garlic, tomatoes, and celery with lots of olive oil, added a few liters of white wine, brought it to a rolling boil, then tossed in shrimp, crab, and lobster with plenty of saffron to give color and body to the soup. Once the soup had attained a silky consistency and a golden sheen, they threw in the fish, including heads, and let it simmer for a few minutes on low heat.

Fewer people agree on how to make bouillabaisse than on the recipe for the perfect martini, though there is consensus that it tastes better if it includes the rascasse, a spiky creature, mostly head, also known as the scorpion fish. Some of the restaurants Angela, Cyril, and I cruised that afternoon boasted of using rascasse in their bouillabaisse, but what convinced us was the family eating on the quay. With napkins stuffed into their collars, mother, father, grandma, and three children attacked a basin of bouillabaisse as big as a washtub. Clearly these people would never accept less than the real thing.

A traditional dockside bouillabaisse, 1910s

We took a table next to them. Assuming we were all agreed, I said, *"Bouillabaisse pour tous les trois, s'il vous plait."*

Cyril harrumphed. "You don't mind if I order my meal?" he said stonily. After staring at the soup-spotted menu, he said, *"Je voudrais le poulet rôti et frites."*

The waiter raised his eyebrows. Chicken and chips, in a seafood restaurant? As long as he lived, he would never understand these *rosbifs* (Brits).

More than thirty years later, sitting in a Paris where, at the time of that earlier trip, I'd never remotely imagined living, the taste of that bouillabaisse came back to me.

The few Paris restaurants that advertised the dish served up a couple of fish fillets in a dish of sludgy pumpkin-colored soup. Bouillabaisse didn't flourish beyond sight of the Mediterranean. It needed sun, garlic, oil, and, above all, rascasse.

Our friend Tim was in town from Australia. A few years ago, he and I had made a memorable expedition one Saturday morning to buy a Matisse as a gift for his wife.

"How would you feel about running down to the Riviera for bouillabaisse?" I asked.

He didn't hesitate. "Love it!"

A week later, we were rocketing across France, headed for Sète.

What a contrast to my first trip, in our old VW. Then, we had stopped overnight in little pensions and, on a few occasions, even pitched our tents at a campsite. Cyril, inevitably a former Boy Scout and member of his university trekking team, shamed us with his taut guy ropes, drum-tight canvas, and state-of-the-art sleeping bag.

Back then, the trip took a week. Now, three hours after climbing aboard the TGV at the Gare de Lyon, Tim and I stepped off into the briskly breezy but sunbright streets of Sète.

A few apartment blocks had replaced buildings demolished by wartime bombing, and pleasure boats rather than trawlers lined the canals. Otherwise, little had changed. Walking to our hotel, we found the street taken over by a market and wove the last hundred meters through stalls selling crimson tomatoes, piles of onions, skeins of garlic, and giant oysters the size of coffee bowls.

By the time we reached the harbor, an hour later, our appetites were sharp. The dockside restaurants looked just as they had in the 1970s, down to the same ocean-blue awnings, tables spilling onto the cobbles, and menus under glass, all advertising, in four or five languages, the true, real, and genuine bouillabaisse.

"Do you remember which one you ate at?" Tim asked.

"Not really."

We chose one almost at random. "Let's try the lunch menu here," I said. "If it's good, we can come back tonight for bouillabaisse."

We ordered the *plateau de fruits de mer*, served on the traditional steeple-shaped wire rack. Its five ascending terraces held oysters, shrimp, crab, a lobster, mussels, and the saltwater crayfish called langoustines. On the side were bowls of aioli—garlic mayonnaise—and the mixture of red wine vinegar and chopped shallots that accompanies oysters everywhere in France.

"Not bad," Tim said, cracking a lobster claw. "I wonder if their bouillabaisse is as good."

We buttonholed the waiter for information. He in turn called the owner over. I explained our search.

"M'sieur, I assure you, we serve *le vrai bouillabaisse. Le vrai de vrai.*"

He pointed to a color photograph on the menu. It showed a tureen of deep red soup flanked by small rounds of toast, a pile of grated Gruyère cheese, and a dish of the chili-flavored mayonnaise called *rouille*— literally "rust." Next to it, a platter was heaped with whole cooked fish, crabs, and other shellfish.

"But this is just *soupe au poisson*," I said.

Any large restaurant in France served the same dish. You spread *rouille* on a crouton of toast, heap on some cheese, float it in the soup, then try to scoop it out before the bread becomes soggy and disintegrates down the front of your shirt. The addition of fried fish changed it not at all.

The owner looked stung. "Not at all, m'sieur. Note the fish." He pointed to the heaped platter. "*Saint Pierre, grondin, lotte . . .*"

"Rascasse?"

He looked uncertain, darted back into the kitchen, and returned a few moments later.

"Our chef tells me that, regrettably, the rascasse is not always available. Nonetheless, we stand by our claim that this is the authentic bouillabaisse Sètoise."

"Bouillabaisse Sètoise? Then there are others?"

"Of course, m'sieur. Bouillabaisse Marseillaise, Bouillabaisse Italienne, Bouillabaisse Espagnol . . ." Not forgetting, I thought, North Sea Bouillabaisse.

So what had I eaten all those years ago? I remembered a single dish of red earthenware, from the depths of which we dredged shrimp, mussels, crab claws, and dripping gobbets of fish. Perhaps the chef had been from Marseilles or even Barcelona or Genoa—quite possible in this cosmopolitan town. Had I eaten Spanish or Italian bouillabaisse rather than the Sètoise version? Or had the years merely blurred the edges of memory, so that what I remembered and what I ate no longer coincided?

If I did serve the dish as part of my banquet, clearly I would have to invent a version of my own that exhibited the qualities I remembered from that first delirious *grande bouffe*.

•　　•　　•

After lunch, Tim and I took a stroll through the narrow streets running up to the mountain that towered behind the town. Big plane trees shaded park benches where old men drowsed and mothers rocked babies in their prams. In one square, we found a flea market, as sleepy as the rest of the town. Like *brocanteurs* all over France, the vendors had brought folding tables and picnic lunches. They lingered over their cheese and red wine, hoping somebody might show interest in their chipped plates, rusty tools, and piles of old magazines.

I noticed Tim was looking a little green.

"Could we find a café?" he asked.

"You feel like a coffee?"

"Not exactly."

At the first café, he bolted for the toilets before we'd even sat down. He returned ten minutes later, even paler.

"I need to go back to the hotel," he said. Something from that *plateau de fruits de mer* had given him a savage case of Sètoise stomach.

By nightfall, he was a little better, though still shaky. Though I'd waited for the same bug to hit me, it never did. I felt fine.

"Don't let me stop you," he said. "You came here to eat bouillabaisse. You should do it."

An hour later, I was back at the dockside. I chose a restaurant at the end of the row and sat down. The waiter handed me a menu. There they were, all the usual suspects: *plateau de fruits de mer, soupe au poisson, langoustines, huitres*—and, of course, bouillabaisse.

"*Je vous écoute,*" said the waiter, pencil poised—I'm listening . . .

I closed the menu. The very thought of seafood turned my stomach.

"*Poulet rôti.*"

"*D'accord. Et avec ça?*"

"*Frites.*"

"*Oui, m'sieur. Poulet rôti frites.*"

You could hear the exasperation in his voice. Chicken and chips! *Rosbifs!*

Eleven

First Catch Your Elephant

I could eat a horse and chase the driver.

Traditional British saying

Cooking in France has a lot to do with class. That's true of all nations, of course. But in Anglo-Saxon countries, wealth shows itself in the richness of the food—fat, butter, sugar, cream—and in the quantities—steaks that overlap the plate, sandwiches so stuffed with filling that one can't get one's mouth around them,

In France, the richer you are, the leaner and more tender the meat you eat, the whiter the bread, the finer the wines, but the smaller the portions. Bread, wine, and meat are a measure of success. When someone who has lived well falls on hard times, the French say, "He ate his white bread first," while "to eat meat every day" is equivalent to the American "catching the gravy train."

Well into the nineteenth century, protein of any kind was a luxury. The poor subsisted on vegetables and grains, a diet that kept energy low and left them too tired after a working day to protest about the miseries of existence. Vegetarianism has never caught on in France because vegetables are regarded as food for the poor. To eat meat, the leaner the better, signifies prosperity. Dine with any middle-class family and you'll likely be served fatless, flavorless roast veal, with a few green beans and perhaps potato purée, followed by cheese.

Outside the cities, the rule of meat with every meal relaxes somewhat, and the definition broadens to include parts of the animal at which city dwellers would turn up their noses.

This point was illustrated by the experience of a family in the country that, having lost its money, decided to economize by firing the cook.

"We're terribly sorry," the wife explained. "It's just that food has become so expensive."

Relieved she wasn't being dismissed for incompetence, the cook said, "But madame, you should have told me! Give me a few weeks. I can save at least enough money from the housekeeping to pay my wages."

She began in the fields and roadsides near the house, scanning the shoulders for snails, picking the arugula and dandelion that grew wild, as well as herbs such as marjoram, chives, and mint. The leaves went into salads, the stalks into stocks and soups, while anything left over was dried to use later.

At the market, she ignored the best fruit and vegetables. Bruised apples and overripe tomatoes were not only cheaper, and sometimes free, but their ripeness made them more suitable for sauces and purées. At the butcher's, she chose cheaper cuts that could be stewed or braised. She also insisted that the butcher wrap the bones and trimmings and add anything that his less frugal clients had left behind. ("For the dogs," she told him, though nobody was fooled.) Bones and scraps were roasted for the fat, then boiled to make stock for soups—all but the suet, the hard white fat from around lambs' kidneys. That was minced raw and substituted for butter to make particularly rich pastry and puddings.

A chicken became a challenge: What part of it *couldn't* be used? By pounding the breast meat into paillards; stewing the legs, thighs, and wings in red wine for coq au vin; and using the bones for soup, a bird could be stretched for three meals, whereas, roasted, it did for only one.

She reserved the livers until she had enough for a terrine. The heart and other edible organs, after being boiled in the stock, were preserved in the skimmed fat. Called *gésiers*, these meaty lumps made a tasty addition to salads. So did the tender "oysters" on either side of the backbone. There's a sneer of peasant superiority in the traditional name for these nuggets: *sot-l'y-laisse*— literally "the stupid leave them."

No matter how provident, one part of the chicken she might have hesitated to use was the feet. In her second book of recipes, *Aromas and Flavors of Past and Present*, Gertrude Stein's companion Alice B. Toklas included Chicken Stuffed with Seafood. It begins, "This recipe calls for a fine chicken with all accessories, including neck, liver, gizzard, tips of wings, and feet." The editor suggested that "and feet" be dropped. Toklas responded, "If you have not the habit of seeing and using the feet, do not be discouraged but do as all continentals do; remember that gelatine is made from feet." Not only did Toklas insist that the feet be included. She described in detail how to remove the claws and skin before they went into the pot.

What else do the stupid leave? Quite a lot, as it happens, particularly when the animal is a cow or pig. The shrewd country housekeeper cooks almost every part, including liver, kidney, brains, bone marrow, and tongue. The hog is a particularly rich source. After the tender parts have been eaten fresh, the remaining joints are cured with salt and sugar, or air-dried to become ham or bacon. Smaller pieces of meat are minced with the fat to make sausages, the intestines providing casings. Ears can be boiled until soft and gelatinous, then either sliced and fried crisp as an addition to salads, or split, stuffed, and served with *sauce gribiche*, a mixture of pickles and capers in a cream thickened with hard-boiled eggs. The boast of Chicago meat-packers "We use everything except the squeal" was learned from the French pork butcher.

Other animals produce just as rich a harvest. Veal bones, called *os à moelle* (marrow bones), are sawed into rounds and baked. Then the marrow is spooned onto toast and sprinkled with *fleur de sel*, the dust-fine "flower of the salt" skimmed from the topmost layer of the pans where seawater is evaporated. *Ris de veau*, or sweetbreads, the sheep's thymus gland, are a gourmet treat when sautéed with walnuts. So is a whole veal kidney in mustard sauce.

Tripe, the stomach lining of a cow, is popular in Normandy, where they prepare it in a brown savory sauce. In Lyon, France's capital of good eating, it appears in a dish called *tablier de sapeur*—sapper's apron. Sappers were the military engineers who tunneled under enemy fortifications to plant explosives. They wore protective aprons of cowhide as thick as the slabs of tripe used in this dish, which are marinated, stewed, then breaded and fried.

Admittedly, there are some things even the French won't eat.

The Roman relished dormice cooked with honey and poppy seeds, but though French fields swarm with the little rascals, no restaurateur has yet been tempted. Another Roman delicacy, testicles, doesn't appear on many menus either, at least in Europe, though it's worth watching the documentary *Long Way Round*, which follows actors Ewan McGregor and Charley Boorman on their motorcycle circumnavigation of the world, to see their faces when, invited to dinner in a Mongolian yurt, they are confronted with a bubbling cauldron of balls.

Some times are so hard, however, that the old rules no longer apply. For a period in 1870 and 1871, even wealthy Parisians would have relished a fat dormouse and eaten testicles with appetite. They *did* devour horse, dog, rat, cat, yak, bear, and elephant. What drove them to this extreme? And how did chefs make such animals edible? The answers constitute one of the most curious stories in the history of cookery.

A t times, as I planned my feast and scoured the country for ingredients, I was made aware, by surprising acts of generosity, that many of the French gourmets to whom I spoke regarded the project as more than just an intellectual exercise. To them, I was reaffirming an ancient and honorable tradition.

Celebrating an occasion with a banquet is deeply established in the French character. Until the 1920s, it was usual to hold a banquet to celebrate a child's first communion or confirmation, as well as a wedding or engagement. A feast might also be staged for political reasons—to celebrate a military victory, or the anniversary of one, or as a tribute to a military or political leader on his retirement.

Very occasionally, patriots chose to display, by means of a *repas*, the superiority of their national way of life. One such meal—perhaps the most famous in French history—took place in 1871, after the nation's worst military defeat.

In July 1870, a festering rivalry between Emperor Napoleon III and the kingdom of Prussia erupted into war. Sadly for France, the emperor, nephew of Napoleon Bonaparte, had inherited none of his uncle's military genius. The army of Prussia, efficiently commanded and well armed, overran the French in its first battle and took Napoleon prisoner. While he haggled over the terms of surrender, the Prussians besieged Paris.

The siege lasted five months, during which no person or animal could get into or out of the city. As artillery battered the outskirts, foreign journalists kept their readers up-to-date by photographically reducing their reports onto microfilm. These were loaded into hot-air balloons launched from the heights of Montmartre. Winds carried the Montgolfiers, as they were known, south to Tours and Poitiers, where the letters were re-trieved, restored to readable size, and posted.

For a while, the army also tried homing pigeons,

until the Prussians brought in hawks to take them down. But the greatest threat to the birds came not from Prussians but hungry Parisians. "It's impossible to find beef or mutton without queueing at the market," complained the abbot of Saint-André, vicar of Saint- Augustin, who obviously liked his food, "and the butchers cheat us by raising prices."

"The slugs are very good tonight."

As beef, chicken, and lamb disappeared, the government, ignoring the decree of Pope Gregory III that it was a "filthy and abominable custom," urged Parisians to eat horse. By chance, *boucheries chevalines* (horse butchers) had appeared for the first time in France just a few years before, signifying their presence, then as now, by a gilded horse's head above their door. Parisians ate seventy thousand horses during the siege. Even the emperor succumbed. Two thoroughbreds, a gift from Czar Alexander II, provided a number of meals for the imperial court.

Once all the horses were used up, it was the turn of Paris's estimated twenty-five thousand cats, followed by dogs, then rats. Rat meat was lean, and a little tasteless, but perfectly edible if well seasoned. The poor already considered it a delicacy, as did sailors, who fattened rats with biscuit crumbs as an alternative to salt pork and beef. Rat sellers set up in the streets. Cheekily dressed as butchers, they offered to skin and joint the animal to your requirements.

The abbot of Saint-André listed some of the new dishes on offer:

Terrine of rat and donkey meat

Rats in champagne

Stewed rat with Sauce Robert [chest-
nuts, onion, and white wine]

Roasted leg of dog, flanked by baby rats

Young donkey (claiming to be veal)

Dogs' brains (much appreciated)

Dogs' livers grilled with herb butter

Sliced saddle of cat with mayonnaise

Cat stewed with mushrooms

Consommé of horse with millet

Dog cutlets with green peas

For those with a sweet tooth, there were begonias in
syrup and plum pudding made with fat from the marrow
of horse bones.

• • •

During the siege, no restaurant worked more strenuously to maintain standards than Voisin. Though the lace-curtained windows of the little establishment at 261 rue St. Honoré suggested a simple café, its food and wine were famous, and famously expensive. Its waiters included César Ritz, later the business partner of chef Georges-Auguste Escoffier and manager of London's Savoy Hotel, then of the Paris establishment that still bears his name.

Voisin prided itself on defending classic French cuisine against foreign fads. M. Bellanger, the headwaiter, indignantly refused an Englishman who demanded a pudding at Christmas, and was just as short with an American woman who requested simply a salad. That incident probably inspired the scene in the film *Ninotchka*, where Soviet commissar Greta Garbo asks a restaurateur for raw vegetables. "Madame," he says stiffly, "this is a restaurant, not a meadow."

Voisin's chef in 1870 was Alexandre-Étienne Choron. Only thirty-two, he came from northern France, so was no stranger to unpromising ingredients. The specialty of his hometown, Caen, was *tripes à la Caen* (tripe in a savory meat sauce), traditionally served on a metal dish suspended above hot coals.

Choron knew his clientele would expect more than horse, cat, or rat. In December, his patience was rewarded when the zoo, the Jardin d'Acclimatation, announced it could no longer feed its animals and reluctantly offered them for sale as livestock.

Paris butchers snapped up deer, antelopes, and even bear, all known to be edible. Imaginatively, M. Deboos of the Boucherie Anglaise on boulevard Haussmann bought a yak. Under all that hair, it was, after all, just a kind of buffalo and could pass for beef. At the end of December, he also paid 27,000 francs for two elephants, Castor and Pollux. Not sure how to slaughter them, he hired a sharpshooter named De Vismes to kill them with 33-millimeter steel-tipped explosive bullets.

Killing the zoo animals, 1871

The gourmet community was soon alive with discussion about the relative merits of the various animals as meat. One of the trapped foreign journalists, Thomas Gibson Bowles, wrote that he'd eaten camel, antelope, dog, donkey, mule, and elephant, and of those, he liked elephant the least. Another commentator, Henry Labouchère, reported, "Yesterday, I had a slice of Pollux for dinner. It was tough, coarse and oily. I do not recommend English families to eat elephant as long as they can get beef or mutton." He probably ate the inferior meat from the body of the elephant, which Deboos sold for ten to fourteen francs a pound. More discriminating chefs, including Choron, had already snapped up the tender trunks at three or four times that price.

Some animals defied even Choron's expertise. The zoo offered a hippopotamus at 80,000 francs but found no takers. Who knew if the blubbery beast was even edible? Lions and tigers were also left alone. Nobody wanted the job of killing them. There was a particular revulsion, too, against monkeys. Because Darwin's *On the Origin of Species* had been published in 1859 and the theory of evolution was gaining acceptance, eating monkeys might have seemed like cannibalism, although, ironically, soldiers in the trenches during World War I sarcastically referred to canned beef as "monkey."

Elephant, bear, camel, kangaroo, antelope, wolf, cat, and rat all figured in a legendary midnight Christmas dinner offered by Voisin in December 1870. This was the menu:

STARTERS

Butter, radishes, stuffed Donkey's head, sardines

SOUPS

Purée of Red Beans with croutons

Elephant Consommé

ENTREES

Fried baby catfish. Roasted camel English style

Kangaroo Stew

Bear chops with pepper sauce

ROASTS

Haunch of wolf with venison sauce

Cat, flanked by Rats

Watercress salad

Antelope Terrine with truffles

Cèpes mushrooms Bordelaise style

Green peas with butter

SWEETS

Rice pudding with preserves

DESSERT

Gruyère cheese

With these exotic dishes, the restaurant offered Mouton-Rothschild 1846, Romanée-Conti 1858, Château Palmer 1864, and, as a digestif, Grand Porto 1827—wines sufficiently fine to make even rat palatable.

Choron's skill backfired on him. His clients developed a taste for elephant. After Christmas, Voisin bought the animal of the Botanical Garden for fifteen francs a pound. Elephant trunk in *sauce chasseur* and *Éléphant bourguignon* went on the menu. Even the blood wasn't wasted. Edmond de Goncourt wrote in his diary on New Year's Eve 1870. "Tonight, at the famous Chez Voisin, I found elephant black pudding and I dined"— presumably with pleasure.

Fortunately for any surviving animals, at the end of January 1871, Napoleon capitulated and abandoned his throne. The government and army, in disorder, had fled from what they feared could be a hand-to-hand battle for Paris against the vastly more competent Prussian troops. However, after an orderly victory parade through the conquered city, the Prussians returned home, leaving Paris in the hands of its dazed but elated citizens. In the power vacuum that followed, the more radical Parisians, particularly those who lived in Montmartre, seized the city and proclaimed the Commune—an anarchist community, with total equality for all.

The changed diet forced on Parisians by the siege played a small but decisive role in the political ferment. Once it became acceptable to eat horse, plentiful in a culture where horses hauled almost every load and provided the main means of transport, a rich source of protein was suddenly available to the poor. This brought greater energy and stamina, better health, and the spirit of revolution.

Imagery of the siege even celebrated the importance of horse meat. An allegorical engraving shows Paris as a defiant woman, sword in hand, with the city burning behind her, while, in the sky, hawks attack a pigeon. She's supporting a shield with eight symbols of the siege: a flaming torch, a balloon, a pigeon, a sword, a set of manacles, an artillery shell, the Croix de Genève (or Red Cross, founded only seven years earlier), and a horse's head. A caption lets the horse itself explain, acquiescing in its own sacrifice. "I have been besieged in Paris, and have fed it."

I t's very French that one of the events most remembered about the siege of Paris was the night the patrons of Voisin ate camel, wolf, and elephant. The Voisin banquet was not simply a culinary event but a social and political one. Significantly, the menu is headed "99th

Day of the Siege." It made the point that Paris remained defiant.

Much as I admired the French, both for their patriotism and their culinary skill, I couldn't help being a little suspicious about this famous feast. Given that the meal was, in part, an act of propaganda, how seriously should we take the menu? Did they eat what was claimed?

Some dishes sound authentic. A stew of kangaroo is one of the few ways to eat this muscular animal. The tail makes a tasty soup, and the rump is as good as venison, but the remaining meat is so tough it's usually ground up for pet food.

Rat is still a delicacy in China, where it was sampled during the 1990s by British TV chef Keith Floyd. He found it "not in any way repugnant. It tasted similar to duck." Floyd, who specialized in demonstrating exotic dishes in remote places, also roasted a leg of bear for a series about cooking next to the Arctic Circle. In cooking his Bear Chops with Pepper Sauce, Choron probably followed a similar recipe to Lloyd's, larding the meat with slivers of bacon and inserting pieces of garlic. It tasted, Floyd said, like the best roast pork.

But not even Floyd would have suggested roasting the notoriously tough camel, or serving wolf at all. Modern food writer M. F. K. Fisher published a book called *How to Cook a Wolf*, but in her case, the wolf was metaphorical—a symbol for hunger. She never suggested eating one, although during the time she lived in France, she did develop a taste for pâté made from lark, the songbird whose tongues had been a delicacy at medieval tables.

As for the rest of the Voisin menu, Stuffed Donkey's Head sounds dubious, particularly since it appears, incongruously, among the starters, next to sardines and radishes with butter, both traditional pre-dinner savories. A donkey's head has little edible meat, so the head was probably papier-mâché, perhaps borrowed from a theatrical warehouse, which would have kept it in stock for productions of *A Midsummer Night's Dream*.

Cat Flanked by Rats also sounds suspicious. No chef would place such an unappetizing oddity next to Antelope Terrine with Truffles, clearly a dish of distinction. On the other hand, it would not be beyond the skill of Voisin's kitchen to create a cat and rats in aspic, or in shortcrust, enclosing a *pâté en croûte*.

To have staged such a patriotic event made Voisin more famous than ever. It even opened a branch in New York. Until the original closed in 1930, its customers included kings and princes, as well as the greats of politics and the arts. It no longer served elephant and camel, but "if the owner looks upon you with eyes of favour," wrote one client, "you will be presented by him with a little pink card, folded in two, on which is the menu of a dinner given at Voisin's on Christmas Day 1870."

Choron himself lived until 1924, content to coast on his reputation. Aside from the 1870 dinner, he's best known for sauce Choron, a mayonnaise flavored with tomato and tarragon, which, according to rumor, he invented by accident when he spilled tomato purée into some Béarnaise sauce. About any fakery connected with his famous banquet, however, he had the good sense to keep his mouth shut.

Twelve

First Catch Fire

The story of barbecue is the story of America: settlers arrive on great unspoiled continent, discover wondrous riches, set them on fire and eat them.

Vince Staten, in *Real Barbecue*

As Vatel and Choron realized, a formal dinner must be both a meal and a show. At the banquets they supervised, a dish's appearance meant as much as, if not more than, how it tasted. From Roman times, cooks were valued for their ability to create a meal that was also a spectacle. If my *repas* was to be a true success, it must be at least partly a piece of theatre.

Trimalchio, the party-giver of Petronius's *Satyricon*, mixed food and theatricals on a grand scale. At the feast Petronius describes, a huge pig is carried in.

> *One and all, we expressed our admiration. Presently, Trimalchio, staring harder and harder, ex-*

claimed "What! It's been cooked with its guts still inside? Call the cook."

The cook came and stood by the table, looking crestfallen and saying he had clean forgot.

"What? Forgotten?" cried Trimalchio. "Strip him!" he ordered, reaching for his whip.

We all began to intercede for him, saying, "Accidents will happen. Forgive him this once."

Trimalchio, a smile breaking over his face, told the cook, "Well, as you have such a bad memory, gut the beast now, where we can all see."

With trembling hand, the cook slashed open the animal's belly. Out tumbled quantities of sausages and black puddings made from the pig's organs and entrails. At this, all the servants applauded like one man. The cook was rewarded with a goblet of wine and a silver wreath.

Medieval chefs had to be able to present a cooked swan or peacock in its plumage, and build fragile palaces of spun sugar. Some dishes were no more than party tricks; a huge pie, carried to the table by a team of servants, might prove to be filled with live birds that flew out as it was cut, or a turkey would be stuffed with a chicken, the chicken with a guinea hen, the guinea hen with a spatchcock, the spatchcock with a quail, and so on, down to an ortolan, the smallest edible bird, the size of one's thumb.

These creations, after being paraded for the guests, were placed on show for the commoners to gawk at. Nobody at the royal table actually ate them. But even uneaten, they trumpeted prestige. To have cooks who could prepare such dishes was impressive enough. But to care so little about the cost that you just let them sit there—that showed real wealth.

Fragments of this ostentation live on in our own Thanksgiving and Christmas turkey or sucking pig, served whole, and carved at the table. The classic multi-story wedding cake belongs to the same tradition. With each such cake my father made, he supplied a few small boxes of thin silvery metal, their lids embossed with wedding bells. If a friend or relative couldn't attend the reception, he or she was sent a slice of cake as a souvenir—a distant echo of commoners being invited in to admire the feast. Pieces of royal wedding cake in similar tins turn up occasionally. A survivor from the ill-fated wedding of Prince Charles and Lady Diana sold in 2008 for $1,830.

•　　•　　•

A more flamboyant survival from the days of spectacle is the Piping in the Haggis. This traditionally takes place on the twenty-fifth of January, birthday of Scotland's revered poet, Robert Burns. In a miniature variation on the Roman roasted pig stuffed with its own sausages, haggis is made from a sheep's stomach crammed with oatmeal, onions, spices, and the sheep's chopped kidneys, heart, and liver. This is then steamed until it reaches the consistency of a slightly crumbly meat loaf. It may not excite the appetite of every gourmet, but Burns loved it, and even composed a poem in its honor.

"Address to a Haggis" is the most passionate tribute ever penned to any dish, let alone one made with what American supermarkets call "variety meats" but the British frankly label "offal." Describing haggis as the "great chieftain o' the puddin' race," Burns, writing in dialect, suggests that a true Scot would cheerfully subsist on nothing else:

> Ye Pow'rs wha mak mankind your care,
> And dish them out their bill o' fare,
> Auld Scotland wants nae skinking ware
> That jaups in luggies;
> But if ye wish her gratfu' prayer,
> Gie her a Haggis!

Which translates roughly as:

You powers who make Man your care
And dish them out their bill of fare,
Remember Scotland doesn't care
For gravied dishes.
But if you wish her grateful prayer
Give her a haggis!

At a Burns Night banquet, "Address to a Haggis" is traditionally recited as the dish is paraded around the table, preceded by a bagpiper. After a lengthy dedication—Burns dictates "a grace as lang's my arm"—the host carves it up and serves his guests. This, at least, is how it should go, but as Burns himself remarked, "the best-laid schemes o' mice an' men gang aft agley"—the best-laid plans of mice and men often go awry.

At a Burns Night in an Australian university in the 1960s, a giant haggis was much admired for the way it conformed to Burns's description of juices oozing through the skin: "while thro' your pores the dews distil / Like amber bead." The college chef confided to friends that he'd cooked it in his latest acquisition, an industrial-size pressure cooker. Somebody in the physics department, overhearing, started to explain that a permeable membrane—a sheep's stomach, for example—can absorb an enormous amount of pressure, which has no way to escape. Just then, the chaplain concluded his grace. The college president rose in his formal gown, picked up a carving knife, and cut—

The explosion was audible all over campus. For days, cleaning staff were scraping sheep's entrails off the walls.

For my part, I sympathized.

I once decided to liven up an Australian barbecue by serving a kebab, not on the conventional metal skewer but with the meat impaled on a sword, and carried to the table in flames.

As *shashlik*, this dish had been served in Russian restaurants in the 1920s—the *shashka* is a kind of sabre—but became familiar during the 1960s as a specialty of certain American restaurants. Once I'd seen the drawing of a waiter in a white jacket coolly carrying such a flaming sword through a crowd of diners in Chicago's Pump Room, I wouldn't be satisfied until I'd tried it.

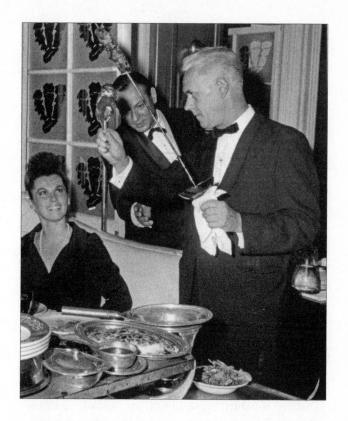

Fencing friends were surprisingly unwilling to lend me their weapons after I told them what I had planned. The old foil that one did find in the back of a closet was both rusty and bent. I removed the worst of the rust, but nothing could be done about the bend. Nor was the point sharp—understandable for a sporting weapon but a problem if you were skewering cubes of lamb.

You have to try impaling meat to realize how long swords are. With most of the meat used up, mine was still only half full. I removed the lamb, now looking a bit bedraggled, and started over, alternating with pieces of onion, green pepper, mushrooms, tomatoes, and squares of bacon.

These filled the sword up satisfactorily, but as I carried it to the barbecue that night, one couldn't escape the alarming realization that it weighed a ton.

As we maneuvered the clumsy object onto the grill, Angela asked, "Are you quite sure about this?"

"Why not? In America, restaurants serve it all the time."

"If you say so."

The meat sizzled satisfactorily as it hit the hot metal. I looked across the lawn to our guests, on the patio. Well into the third bottle of red, they took little interest in what was happening at the barbecue. This was just as well, since, when I tried to turn the sword, the meat stuck to the grill. More alarmingly, the hilt was almost too hot to touch.

I raced back to the kitchen looking for something to insulate my hand. Angela called after me, "I wouldn't leave it too long." The tomatoes and mushrooms, now cooked through, were softening, while the meat was still half raw.

Two pot holders protected my hands while I lifted the sword off the flames. As I held out the now-drooping blade, its original bend accentuated by the weight of the meat, Angela doused the length of it with brandy. A better cognac would have burned with more discretion, but rather than waste my Courvoisier, I'd bought the fearsome local spirit, Château Tanunda, advertised as "A True Blue Australian Brew." Its fumes alone would stun a wombat. These rose into the evening air, making my head swim. Angela struck a match and touched it to the kebab. Blue flames raced up and down the blade. In the dusk, it was very effective.

"Coming through!" I called. "Clear the way!"

Raising the sword into the vertical, as I'd seen in magazine illustrations, I headed toward our guests. They looked up with expectation, which turned quickly to alarm. They tell me I was a frightening sight, advancing out of the darkness, holding aloft an object wreathed in blue flames that didn't so much flicker as roar, lighting up not only our garden but those of the houses on either side.

Exclamations of panic came from next door as the brandy, burning like petrol, began to cook the meat all over again, spitting drops of burning fat. In a bushfire, gum trees exploded in a similar crown of fire as the eucalyptus oil in the leaves vaporized and ignited. Our friends had seen this on TV but never in a suburban backyard. Even on this miniature scale, it was alarming. Instinctively, they shrank back.

Meanwhile, hot juice and alcohol trickled down the sword, spilled over the hilt, and soaked the pot holders. They started to smolder, then ignited with a whoosh . . .

I still don't know what went wrong," I said the next morning as I tossed the charred pot holders into the garbage, followed by my shirt with the burned cuffs.

"I think I do." Angela was studying the Pump Room advertisements. "This sword isn't the same as yours."

She was right. In the one carried by the waiter, the cuplike guard, meant to protect the fencer's hand in a fight, faced upward. Now I looked more closely, I saw that these were not authentic swords but large skewers made to resemble them. Any juices or brandy trickling down the blade were caught and held in the cup. I'd bet, too, that some sort of insulation prevented heat from traveling from the blade to the hilt.

Just then, the phone rang. It was one of our guests.

"Best bloody barbie any of us can remember," he said. "That sword! Fuckin' incredible! Never seen anything like it. Can we borrow it? We want to do the same thing at our place next week."

All this came back to me as I mulled over a suggestion made at a dinner party for some friends from Charente. Marie-Dominique's family originated in this region on the Atlantic coast, which produces most of the shellfish for France. The walled garden of our summer house, in the fishing town of Fouras, had been the setting for some mammoth seafood feasts.

"If you're looking for forgotten culinary experiences," said one of our guests, "what about an *éclade*? I can't remember the last time anyone held one."

"And no wonder," said his wife. "When you tried it, you almost set fire to our roof."

"That's not a bad idea," I said. Not noticing Marie-Dominique's warning glance, I continued, rashly, "You're right—it's a dying tradition. I've always wanted to do one. And you're all invited."

When the last guest left, Marie-Dominique said, "You really intend to do an *éclade*?"

"Why not?"

"Because it's dangerous, difficult, time-consuming, dirty—and you've always told me you don't like *moules*."

She was partly right about the *moules*. After the big, meaty, green-lipped mussels of the warm Pacific, it's hard to relish the small black-shelled variety that's almost the only kind available in France. Called *bouchots*, they're grown on logs driven into cold estuarine water at the tide line, mostly along the coast of the English Channel and the North Sea.

The French, however, don't share my dislike. A 2011 survey revealed that *moules frites* (stewed mussels with a side order of fries) was the nation's second most popular dish, preceded only by *magret de canard* (grilled duck breast) and followed by another interloper, North African couscous.

The surprise at this fact was general, and a little embarrassed, on the same scale as that in Britain when it was found that the favorite national nosh was no longer roast beef and Yorkshire pudding but the Indian dish chicken tikka masala, made from cubes of chicken roasted in a tandoor, or clay oven, and served in a creamy curry sauce.

Even worse, mussels, historically, are a favorite dish of the Belgians, whom the French consider to be irredeemably dumb. Calling action movie star Jean-Claude

Van Damme "The Muscles from Brussels" was not only a neat pun, but an implied suggestion that, being Belgian, he isn't too bright.

Mussels would never have figured on such a list ten years ago, in part because they are a chore to prepare. They're more shell than flesh, so it takes a bucket to make a meal. One has to remove any with broken shells, rip off the "beards" with which the mussels moor themselves to the rocks, scrape away the sea slime and tiny limpets, then soak them two or three times in freshwater to rinse out salt and sand. Who but the Belgians, imply the French, could be bothered?

But the *moule* invasion had been taking place for some time, creeping across Picardy as the German armies advanced in 1914, bearing down on Paris, and

Farming mussels

just as scantly noticed by Parisians, who, except when planning their August holidays, took little interest in life outside the *périphérique*.

Once they looked around, Parisians realized the pesky black mollusks were everywhere. Oven-ready trays of *moules* "stuffed" with bread crumbs and swimming in butter had become a feature in supermarkets and as starters in restaurants. At the annual Grande Braderie, France's biggest flea market, held on the first weekend of September in Lille, a little over a hundred kilometers from Brussels, it became customary to pig out on mussels and fries, washed down with beer. Five hundred tons of mussels were consumed over the Braderie weekend, and thirty tons of fries. Drifts of shells build up waist-high in the city squares, monuments to appetite, and also advertisements for restaurants, who competed to have the largest heaps.

Moules, it seems, share a characteristic with foods as different as spareribs and truffles. If you haven't eaten too many, you haven't eaten enough. They also appeal to what the French call *nostalgie de la boue*—the urge occasionally to play in the mud. Even among today's sophisticated holiday makers, eating *moules frites* with their fingers gives a sense of slumming. Esplanades along the Channel coast are thick with trippers strolling in the sun with cardboard dishes of *moules frites*. They have even adopted the Belgian method of eating them using a set of shells as pincers to pluck out the meat, which makes the *moules* perfect finger food.

The cutting edge of the *moule* invasion was Léon de Bruxelles. Opened in 1867, Léon Van Lancker's Brussels restaurant featured *moules special*, with *frites* and beer. In 1989 his grandson Rudy brought Léon to Paris. Today, there are sixty-one branches of Léon de Bruxelles across France, selling eight tons of mussels a day. You can have them cooked traditionally in white wine, or with Roquefort cheese, Madras curry sauce, and in the style of Provence, the Ardennes, or Dijon. But even Léon doesn't have the courage to offer them Charentaise style, *éclate*—exploded.

That rash act was left to me.

G athering your own ingredients for a dish is one of the hallmarks of the true cook. The supermarket is no substitute for a street merchant, who lets you pick and prod, and, in France at least, will lecture on the best methods of preparing what you buy. How much more exciting, then, to search for food in the wild, to hunt and gather, and to sever with your own hands the mystical link between an object and the earth in which it has grown.

Or so I told myself when, late one autumn, I crawled on hands and knees, cursing under my breath, through a forest on the edge of the Atlantic and—avoiding centipedes, wood lice, and those areas around the trees watered and fertilized by local dogs — scrabbled up handfuls of the dry pine needles that carpeted the ground, which I then stuffed into hundred-liter black plastic garbage bags.

Whose dumb idea had it been to stage an *éclade*? Had I really been so stupid?

When I got back to Fouras with two bulging bags, our garden was seething with activity. Paper plates and napkins, jugs of wine, and baskets of sliced baguette covered the big table under the grape arbor. Nearby, a garbage can stood ready to receive the shells.

In the center of the garden, well away from the trees and anything that might catch fire, we'd assembled the antique table-tennis table that usually sat in the laundry room, gathering dust and cobwebs. On top sat a slab of wood about the area of a coffee table. In the center were hammered four three-inch nails, about an inch apart.

Marie-Dominique and her sister tottered out of the house with a galvanized metal bath brimming with gleaming mussels. A *fournisseur* in the fish market offered, for a small premium, to deliver them cleaned and ready to cook. He used a sort of washing machine to scrub off the worst incrustations, but as a precaution, we'd put them to soak a second time—just as well, since, when we dredged them out, a thin layer of sand remained in the bottom of the bath.

"What now?"

Marie-Dominique took a mussel and leaned it, hinge uppermost, against one nail. She continued until she had a square, then looked at us expectantly.

"Well, come on."

It took the three of us almost an hour to cover the wood with a carpet of gleaming mussels. By then, the guests were arriving. They paused by the table to admire our work. A few tried to help, but it required a sure hand to place the mussels so that they stood upright. If one toppled, a dozen others might also go, like dominoes. Seeing it was not as much fun as it looked, they drifted toward the wine.

The soft summer night descends with stately deliberation on the coast of Charente, so it was almost ten before we opened the bags of pine needles. In handfuls, we laid them evenly on top of the mussels.

When they were a foot deep, I asked, "Isn't that enough?"

Marie-Dominique shook her head. We kept on until both bags were empty and the pile of needles resembled a miniature haystack.

"Come on everyone," she called. "We're ready."

Glasses in hand, our guests clustered around.

Although the *éclade* is complex in preparation and, with luck, spectacular in effect, the theory behind it is simple. Fishermen of a century before improvised the dish as a way to cook *moules* quickly without utensils. They peeled a slab of bark from a cork tree, piled it with mussels, added pine needles, then lit it. The needles burned quickly and intensely, leaving a layer of ash, which they blew away to reveal the mussels burst open by the steam of their juices, with the bonus of a resinous tang from the pine.

As our guests stood well back, Marie-Do, her sister, and I stationed ourselves at the corners of the table. At a nod, we each struck a match and touched it to the needles.

It happened so quickly that, later, nobody could agree on what had gone wrong. Marie-Dominique insisted the mussels were too small. I was sure we'd used too many needles. The summer had been exceptionally dry, making them unusually inflammable. Whatever the reason, the needles acted like the brandy on my disastrous sword kebab. A plume of flame shot into the air, sending our guests recoiling and squealing. One bumped a corner of the table, and the heap of burning needles slowly began to topple. Sparks whirled up, threatening to carry the fire into our neighbors' gardens.

It didn't, though it was a damned close-run thing, and I only just stopped someone from turning the hose on the *éclade* and ruining it completely.

Once the fire died down and the ash was fanned away, we found that the mussels were cooked through. Well, mostly anyway. Those around the edges didn't so much burst as vaporize, the shells turning to ash. Elsewhere, in patches, the heat had been too mild, so the mussels remained uncooked. But where the clustering effect protected them from the worst of the heat, they gaped invitingly, their meat juicy, resinous, and quite pleasant, if you didn't mind ash grating between your teeth.

Next day, our friends rang to thank us. As I should have anticipated, they reacted exactly as the guests at my *shashlik* barbecue had done. "*Quel spectacle! Etonnant, vraiment.*" Everyone agreed it had been, literally, a roaring success.

But that table-tennis table never gave a decent bounce again.

Thirteen

First Catch Your Socca

Here silver olives shine
On terra-cotta earth
And fields of lavender
In the still, burning air
Have all their scent distilled.
The sky's so primary blue
The halftones disappear:
Each color its most true,
Each object its most clear.

May Sarton, *Provence*

A t the end of its five-hour journey to the farthest southern corner of France, the railway line swings sharply east to run along the Mediterranean in the direction of Italy.

Waking from a doze, I blinked at a panorama of dark-blue sea washing over jagged rocks, brick-red. "I'd never seen rocks like them," my mother-in-law, Claudine, had told me, the memory of her first visit still vivid after more than sixty years.

Back then, this had been *Le Train Bleu* (the Blue Train), and as famous as the Orient Express. Between 1922 and 1947, it collected passengers off the boat at Calais and carried them in luxury to Ventimiglia, on the Italian Riviera, stopping on the way at Paris, Dijon, Marseilles, Toulon, Saint-Raphaël, Cannes, Juan-les-Pins, Antibes, Nice, Monaco, Monte Carlo, and Menton.

Film stars, industrialists, and diplomats were regular passengers. Professional gamblers heading for Monte Carlo played high-stakes bridge in its club car while *poules de luxe* loitered, poised to fleece the winners of their loot. A beautiful woman traveling alone on the Blue Train was instantly cloaked in mystery, usually well deserved. Maurice Dekobra gave such women a label when he called his 1927 bestseller *The Madonna of the Sleeping Cars*.

Artists loved the Blue Train. Director Michael Powell, who grew up in a hotel his father owned in Antibes, celebrated it in *The Red Shoes*. Moira Shearer's Vicky Page, doomed by her love of dancing, even dies under its wheels. In the 1930 film *Monte Carlo*, Jeanette MacDonald sings "Beyond the Blue Horizon" as she races across France toward the only blue that really counts: the blue of the Côte d'Azur.

In 1924, Darius Milhaud wrote a ballet called *Le Train Bleu* for Sergei Diaghilev, a frequent passenger.

The script was by another regular, Jean Cocteau, with costumes by a third, Coco Chanel, and a backdrop by a fourth, Pablo Picasso. Into his script, Cocteau slyly incorporated details of a Riviera holiday's special pleasures. Illicit lovers, instead of sneaking in and out of bedrooms, could retire, as do couples in the ballet, to the cabanas that lined the beaches of the better hotels.

During 1937 and 1938, on the grounds of the Hotel du Cap, Marlene Dietrich dallied in such tents with movie mogul and diplomat Joseph Kennedy. When Kennedy's twenty-year-old son, John, paid a visit for a ball, Marlene ensured that the event would never be forgotten by the future president of the United States. As they danced to that year's big hit, Cole Porter's "Begin the Beguine," she slipped her hand into his pants.

A ren't you going to include Provence?" Marie-Dominique had asked as she reviewed my progress with plans for the banquet.

"I did," I said. "Remember the bouillabaisse?"

"But you didn't eat bouillabaisse. You just tried to eat it. Also, Provence is huge. The Côte d'Azur is just part of it."

She was right, of course. Most of the Mediterranean coast of France from the Italian border halfway to Spain could loosely be called Provence, since it had once been a province of Rome, hence the name. And while Provence might, technically, end where the Alpes-Maritimes rise behind Cannes, others will tell you it continues north to Avignon, 115 miles up the Rhone. No Mason-Dixon Line marks the border. Provence isn't a region so much as a state of mind.

For more than a century, Britons and Americans have dreamed of living out their fantasies in the warm south. In the 1990s, British writer Peter Mayle's *A Year in Provence* and its follow-up, *Toujours Provence*, sold in the hundreds of thousands. Mayle wrote about his attempts to convert a house, frustrated at every turn by the Provençal people, whom he draws as well-meaning but disorganized, inclined to stop work for extended lunches, prone to hypochondria and superstition, friendly toward those outsiders who accommodate their ways but stubbornly resistant to change.

No Anglo-Saxon reader was discouraged by Mayle's difficulties. Rather, they made them even keener to find a tumbledown villa and hire their own maddening Frenchmen to fix it up. Today, every hilltop village below 43° north echoes to the pounding of hammers and the whine of saws as ancient houses become holiday hideaways with four bedrooms, each with a bathroom en suite. The noise of construction competes with that of onions and tomatoes being chopped, garlic crushed, and all three sizzling in olive oil. Louder still is the clatter of keyboards as would-be Mayles document each nail driven and meal cooked, in the hope that they too will hatch a bestseller.

"The rich are very different to you and I," Scott Fitzgerald famously is said to have told Ernest Hemingway.

"Yes," Hemingway replied. "They have more money."

More important, they have more houses. The history of how Provence was colonized by foreigners is actually the history of houseguests.

After World War I, the Côte d'Azur languished. Co-opted during the war as convalescent homes, the great hotels, the Negresco and the Carlton, the latter with perkily pointed cupolas inspired by the breasts of courtesan La Belle Otero, fell on hard times. A significant part of their clientele had been Russian aristocrats and their servants, so numerous that Nice built an Orthodox cathedral for them. But the 1917 revolution swept them away. Grand Dukes, once the hotels' best clients, now worked for them as waiters and doormen or drove cabs.

Postwar Provence was abandoned to its original inhabitants. "At that time," said American expatriate Gerald Murphy, "no one ever went near the Riviera in summer. The English and the Germans who came down for the short spring season closed their villas as soon as it began to get warm in May. None of them ever went in the water, you see."

Colette, author of *Chéri* and *Gigi*, bought a house in the fishing village of St. Tropez in 1925 with her third husband, Maurice Goudeket. Other than a few painters, no outsiders lived there. "In the evenings, in the genuine bars," wrote Goudeket, "the young people of the country would dance to the tunes of mechanical pianos, the boys with each other and the girls with each other."

At the same time, Gerald Murphy and his wife, Sara, visited Cole Porter at his villa near Antibes, and fell in love with the emptiness of the area. A nearby beach was so little used that a meter of seaweed blanketed the sand. The Murphys excavated a corner in which to enjoy the sun, and later bought a house nearby, christening it Villa America. It became an ad hoc hostel for their creative friends. Eric Newby credits the Murphys with transforming the Côte d'Azur.

> *Without realizing it, they had invented a new way*
> *of life (or one which, if it ever existed, had not done*
> *so since pre-Christian times), and the clothes to go*
> *with it. Shorts made of white duck, horizontally-*
> *striped matelots' jerseys and white work caps bought*
> *from sailors' slop shops became a uniform. From*
> *now on, the rich, and ultimately everyone else in*
> *the northern hemisphere, wanted unlimited sun, the*
> *sea, sandy beaches or rocks to dive into it from, and*
> *the opportunity to eat al fresco.*

In 1923, when Coco Chanel stepped ashore in Cannes from the yacht of her lover the Duke of Westminster, her all-over tan and simple, comfortable clothing signaled a trend. "I think she may have invented sunbathing," sighed Prince Jean-Louis Faucigny-Lucinge. "At that time, she invented everything."

Riviera style and the rediscovery of the sun induced rhapsodies of vanity and self-love in the pale intellectuals of the north. American composer Ned Rorem, staying with the Comtesse Marie-Laure de Noailles in her Mallet-Stevens-designed villa at Hyères, wrote in his diary, "In my canary-yellow shirt (from Chez Vachon in St. Tropez), my golden legs in khaki shorts, my tan sandals, and orange hair, I look like a jar of honey." That evening, the surrealist poet Paul Éluard and his wife came to dinner. "He is deeply suntanned," noted Rorem, "(they had spent the afternoon on Ile de Levant, the land of nudists)." After dinner, they sat on the terrace and Éluard read to them from Baudelaire. As Wordsworth wrote of the French Revolution, "Bliss was it in that dawn to be alive, but to be young was very heaven."

S cott and Zelda Fitzgerald discovered the Riviera through the Murphys. Between April and October 1928, they lived in the Murphys' Paris apartment, next to the Luxembourg Garden, and spent the summer at Villa America, part of a revolving cast of celebrity freeloaders that included Pablo Picasso, Man Ray, Cole Porter, John Dos Passos, Dorothy Parker, and Jean Cocteau.

So I was in good company when I invited myself to spend the weekend with our friend Charles. He owns homes around the world, including one on the heights of the Alpes-Maritimes above Cannes.

Since life at Villa America inspired Fitzgerald to write *Tender Is the Night*, I used the train trip to refresh myself on houseguest etiquette by rereading it, in particular the dinner party scene that ends in an extravagant gesture by the manic Nicole.

> *Rosemary watched Nicole pressing upon her mother a yellow evening bag she had admired, saying, "I think things ought to belong to the people that like them"—and then sweeping into it all the yellow articles she could find, a pencil, a lipstick, a little note book, "because they all go together."*

Though Fitzgerald describes the flowers at that

dinner, the clothes, the conversation, and, naturally, the booze (Veuve Clicquot champagne), he doesn't mention the food. Whatever Americans went to the Riviera for, it wasn't to eat.

Not so the French. Colette, described by Janet Flanner as "an artistic gourmet in a country where eating ranks as an art," embraced the local cuisine, particularly its fiery garlic, which can burn like chili. Most of her meals, wrote Maurice Goudeket, began with

> *a crust of bread dipped in olive oil, lavishly*
> *rubbed in garlic and sprinkled with coarse salt.*
> *Cooked garlic seasoned every dish and in addition,*
> *throughout the whole meal, Colette ate raw cloves*
> *of it as if they had been almonds. Lunch consisted*
> *of Provençal dishes only: green melons, anchoiade*
> *[anchovies pounded with garlic, oil, and vinegar*
> *and served as a dip with raw vegetables], stuffed*
> *rascasse, rice with favouilles [small green crabs],*
> *bouillabaisse and aioli [garlic mayonnaise].*

Purists accuse the Blue Train of ruining the local cuisine. As tourists flowed in, restaurateurs arrived from Italy, Sicily, and Corsica to feed them. They overwhelmed the less flamboyant local dishes. "Provençal" became shorthand for any dish of pasta or seafood with a sauce of tomato, garlic, onions, and olive oil. The same ingredients, with a few olives, hard-boiled eggs, and anchovies, constituted so-called salade Niçoise—salad in the style of Nice. Anyone who has suffered this cuisine will not be surprised to hear that a local remedy for a head cold is water in which you've boiled a rat.

These dishes invariably incorporated herbes de Provence. The curry powder of French cuisine, this mixture is just as imprecise about its ingredients. Thyme, oregano, and rosemary are standard, but after that, it's a question of what's on the shelf: marjoram, basil, tarragon, sage, bay, fennel seed, lavender, dill weed, chervil, even mint and orange zest—anything that assaults the nose with an herbal tang. No wonder unscrupulous dope dealers passed off herbes de Provence to their dumber clients as cannabis.

Fortunately, local producers are fighting back. The Co-operative du Producteurs d'Herbes de Provence has opened a shop almost next door to us in Paris, from which they sell a mixture that, they insist, is the only true and authentic herbes de Provence: 26 percent oregano, 26 percent savory, 19 percent thyme, and 3 percent basil. The young man in charge of the shop dismissed supermarket varieties as fakes. "You know where most of their herbs come from?" he hissed. "Poland!"

The Cannes into which I stepped from the TGV was a town I barely recognized. A chill wind, precursor of Provence's annual curse, the mistral, stirred dust along streets that I knew only in film festival time. For those ten days in May, journalists jam the lanes of the old town and Maseratis with Emirate license plates park nose to tail along the Croisette. This was a different Cannes, obviously, with not a Maserati in sight. Maybe the food would be different, too.

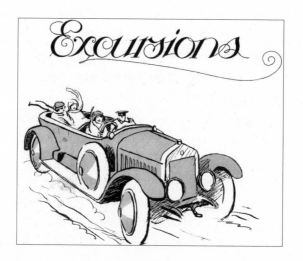

Wedged into Charles's daffodil-yellow sports car, we zoomed away from the station and headed north, into the mountains that climb behind the narrow coastal strip.

"I thought we might have lunch in Mougins," he said.

"At the Moulin, you mean?"

Inwardly, I flinched. At festival time, the Moulin de Mougins is a favored hangout of movie people, with prices to match. Its sea scallops smoked over pine needles and served with black truffle risotto can set you back a sum that, elsewhere, would cover an entire meal.

"Well, I'd prefer somewhere more modest," Charles said, "but if you'd really like . . ."

"No, no. It's fine," I said hurriedly. "Let's slum for a change."

In a large but mostly empty restaurant in Mougins, I had white bean soup enriched with a trickle of truffle oil, followed by a decent lamb stew and crème brûlée. Not a trace of tomato sauce in the entire menu, or of herbes de Provence. To be fair, tomatoes would have struggled here. Almost no vegetation grows on these crags—just sad, stately cypresses and those twisted olive trees that can root in a few handfuls of earth. The rest is rock. Thyme and oregano sprout in the cracks, but you take your life in your hands to harvest them.

We climbed, switchbacking along narrow roads buttressed by dry stone walls, snaking through villages that showed little sign that plastic or steel had ever been invented. Up here, you made do with what the mountains gave you. Rough-hewn chestnut beams might date back to the Middle Ages. Windows were asymmetrical and misshapen, their iron hasps and hinges thick and rusted, hammered out in the local smithy. Frames were carpentered to fit the panes, rather than vice versa. Glass had been more precious than wood.

Charles's home is in the hilltop village of Cabris. Three centuries ago, it was a farmhouse attached to the château of the Marquis de Clapiers-Cabris. Peasants tore down the big house in 1789, hauling away its stones to improve their own homes. All that remains is a crumbling arch, once the grand entrance, and the paved Place Mirabeau that extends to where the cliff drops 1,800 feet toward the Mediterranean.

Cabris

Just before dinner, we walked to the edge and looked down. Below, terraces hardly bigger than a living room sustained olive trees and fruit trees. Beyond, the coastal plain spread to the darkening Mediterranean, the ocean that, to the ancients, was the middle of the earth.

"When the mistral blows," Charles said, "the air clears. You can see Corsica, a hundred and ten miles away. People from the village come up here to watch."

Maybe they are also looking for Antoine de Saint-Éxupéry. From childhood, the pilot-philosopher who wrote *The Little Prince* spent summers in Cabris. In July 1944 he took off from Corsica, flying a P-38 Lightning, and never returned. Some wreckage and the remains of a body were recovered off Marseilles. Most assume he chose to quench his increasing depression in the Mediterranean's hypnotic blue.

We ate at L'Auberge du Vieux Château. It wasn't a long walk—just next door.

I thought I knew every variation on Kir, but for our aperitif, the chef, Emilie Guetet, produced a new one: champagne and lychee liqueur, with, in the bottom of the glass, a tiny spoonful of *confit de pétales de rose*— rose petal jam. Though tasty, it hovered in that troubled area between refreshment and display, next to the my tai with an orchid in it or sambuca with a flaming coffee bean floating on top. Should we drink it or simply, like a flower arrangement, admire it?

Over the next three hours, we worked our way through a menu of authentic Provençal delicacies, faultlessly prepared on our behalf by Cyril Martin and proprietor Anne Loncle. A soup of locally grown pumpkin was followed by a tiny stuffed squid, accompanied by sautéed zucchini, then a few spoonsful of *boeuf bourguignon* on a tile of oil-fried bread, with a curl of homemade paprika fettuccine, then wedges of goat cheese with a salad of *mâche*. Colette might have preferred more garlic, but in other respects she would have been delighted.

Living well is the best revenge. Dining with my friend and host Charles.

After dinner we walked around town. Nothing in this landscape was soft. It had worn down the Phoenicians, the Romans, the Moors, and within a few centuries, it would have seen us off, too. Unlike the hot hill towns to the north, in the Luberon or Vaucluse, it resisted romance. Fitzgerald never wrote about it, nor has any movie star bought a house here—for fear, perhaps, of being reminded how little he matters. Its only cultural associations are French. Saint-Éxupéry's mother and widow both retired to Cabris, and the town named a tiny square in his honor. André Gide summered here, preying on its schoolboys but also, to the surprise of all, fathering a daughter; more proof, like that rose confiture in our Kir, of a capacity for the unexpected.

P rovence did have one last surprise for me.

The next day, we drove down to the Saturday market in Antibes. The *halles*, roofed but open-sided, already jostled with shoppers and vendors. Zucchini flowers, so rare in Paris, were heaped everywhere. Hot chilis, too, which offend the Parisian palate. A whiff of herbes de Provence led me to the spice merchant, who sold rosemary, oregano, dill, bay, and mint separately, in their own dishes, next to crimson paprika and yellow turmeric—all the flavors of Provence but each one individual, respected for itself.

At the end of the market, where it opened onto the paved square, I glimpsed flames.

"What's that?"

"Oh, the *socca* man."

I looked blank.

"You don't know *socca*?"

"Should I?"

"Good heavens, yes."

A cart was parked half outside the market. Within a metal hood about the size of the brick ovens used to cook pizza, flames roared from a liquid gas cylinder. Watched by his wife, standing behind a table, the *socca* man poured thin batter onto a wide metal dish attached to a long handle and slipped it in under the flames. The upper surface began to bubble and brown.

"What's in it?"

Madame pointed to a sign hanging on a column.

SOCCA. Farine de Pois Chiche.
Huile d'Olive. Eau. Sel. 3 Euros.

The man slid the pancake onto a square of foil. The top was brown, the underside pale. Madame dusted it with pepper and slashed it into finger-food-size pieces.

I picked one up—it was almost too hot to touch—and munched.

"Wonderful!"

Chickpea flour, olive oil, water, and salt, with a bite of white pepper: Who could have imagined such simple ingredients could taste so good?

"You find *socca* all along this side of the Mediterranean," Charles said. "I'm surprised you never had it before."

So was I. But would it have tasted the same in Paris or London or New York, or even here, during festival time? Probably not. This was something to be eaten with cold stone underfoot, the mistral whipping up dust, and market people crying the merits of their cheese and fish. When time grinds away all of lesser value, this is what remains. "Perfection is achieved, not when there is nothing more to add, but when there is nothing left to take away."

Saint-Éxupéry said that.

Fourteen

First Catch Your Burger

> *VINCENT: You know what they call a Quarter Pounder*
> *with Cheese in Paris? They call it a Royale with Cheese.*
> *JULES: What do they call a Whopper?*
> *VINCENT: I didn't go into Burger King.*
>
> Quentin Tarantino, *Pulp Fiction*

Whatever other ingredients might make up my banquet, it hardly needed emphasizing that the most important dish, the centerpiece, must involve beef.

Veal is the meat of the bourgeoisie, but it's beef they eat for pleasure. For proof, look no further than a recent French TV commercial. A family of horned, black-faced, but otherwise well-dressed, upper-middle-class demons is grilling steaks on an indoor barbecue. With a burst of heavenly music, servants open the double doors to admit their dinner guests: a band of angels preceded by . . . well, he's wearing a tennis sweater, not a robe,

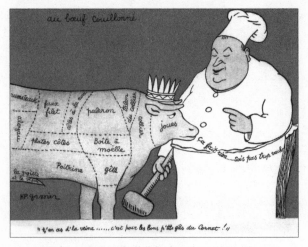

A butcher explains to the bull that he is dying in a good cause

but the crosier he carries and the saintly smile on his bearded face leave little doubt about his—or should that be His?—identity. While angels and devils canoodle and steaks sizzle, the visitor drools over thick slices of pink and tender beef. Yes, friends, it's official: Jesus likes it rare. The ad closes on him dancing with his diabolical opposite number, and the slogan "*Le Boeuf. Le Gout d'Etre Ensemble.*"—"Beef: The Taste of Togetherness."

Meanwhile, news of my interest in attending an ox roast was spreading, though often transformed in the process. A few people thought we were looking for a live animal to cook and offered suitable beasts at markdown prices. Plenty of amateur farmers living on the outskirts of Paris owned cows that, bought in a spasm of enthusiasm—"Imagine, our own fresh milk and cream!"—were eating them into bankruptcy. Their readiness to sacrifice Daisy for cash reminded me of a story that circulated when Australian director George Miller was putting together *Mad Max II*, aka *The Road Warrior*. Since Mel Gibson's Max walks with a limp, Miller thought the character should be accompanied by an equally handicapped dog called Trike, possibly missing an entire leg. A call went out for such an animal— withdrawn after some of the trainers they approached eyed their pack thoughtfully and asked, "How soon would you need it?"

Vegetarianism may have made slight inroads into France, but, at most, a fingernail's grip has grown to a toehold. The soul of any meal remains a joint, filet, or fowl. It arrives at the table in aristocratic solitude, deferentially accompanied by its sauce on the side. Vegetables, if served at all, are smuggled in. Many restaurants don't even identify them, indicating only that the dish is *garni*—garnished. If you ask a waiter about vegetables, he's likely to stare as if you've inquired where he buys his aprons. There is even a theory that learning how to cook meat sparked the birth of civilization. Raw vegetables and meat are hard to chew and difficult to digest. Boiling and roasting softened them. It also encouraged early man to gather round the communal fire and share a meal, the first step in creating a culture.

Scarcely a decade goes by without some scandal connected with beef. Invariably, the French come out winners. The last crisis was the outbreak in Britain of "mad cow" disease in the late 1990s, which led to the European Union's banning the importation of British meat. When asked how bovine spongiform encephalopathy could have stopped magically at the English Channel and not affected their herds, French farmers simply stared at the sky and hummed the "Marseillaise" under their breath. Rumors that infected animals may have been quietly buried at midnight or fed into abattoir furnaces faded away for lack of hard evidence.

The scandal over BSE was as nothing, however, compared to the battle over the introduction into France of the hamburger. On cold winter nights, fast-food entrepreneurs gather their children round their knees and tell them horror stories of what happened in the 1970s when American burger companies, including the mighty McDonald's, tried and, initially, failed to crack the French market.

The hero of that fight was Raymond Dayan, a businessman from North Africa who started as an interior decorator in the United States. While redesigning the home of McDonald's owner Ray Kroc, he persuaded Kroc to assign him the McDonald's franchise for Chicago's North Side. He did so well that he turned his eyes to France, where the company had already attempted to build a chain but had given up in defeat. McDo—as the French call it—gave Dayan a thirty-year license to introduce the Big Mac to France. How poorly they rated his chances is reflected in the terms. Most franchisees paid up to 12 percent of their income to the parent company. Dayan was obligated to remit a mere 1 percent.

Dayan thought he knew why McDonald's had flopped. The company didn't understand how finicky the French were about beef. Not only were its skinny fries an insult to the nation that invented *pommes frites*, but McDo burgers were too fatty for their taste.

He started by changing recipes, even though, strictly speaking, this breached the terms of his franchise. As well as thickening his fries, making the beef patties leaner, adding more mustard to the salad dressing, and selling beer and Evian instead of shakes, Dayan accepted that the French hate standing in line. In the United States, customers queued in orderly fashion. A line in Paris, on the other hand, resembled, as one American wrote, "a triangle, with the base at the place where business is being conducted." A new system of tapes, cords, and "Next client, please" kept his customers in order.

But the real inspiration was in changing the clientele, A burger, fries, and a Coke may be the favorite meal of the U.S. working man, but for the French it was as exotic as chocolate-coated octopus. "You don't find any blue-collar workers or peasants in fast-food restaurants in France," explained the head of a rival chain. "For them, being in a fast-food restaurant is a little like being on the moon."

McDo had placed its restaurants in industrial districts, near railway stations and factories. Dayan moved them to the snobby boulevards such as the Champs-Élysées, next to first-run cinemas and establishments such as Le Drug Store, where trendsetters and taste-makers hung out. Le Drug Store had already proved its influence by introducing the American concept of the

mixed salad. This might combine ham, cheese, croutons, nuts, egg, and even foie gras with its lettuce, all
accompanied by a thick, sweet sauce the menu insisted
on calling "French dressing," even though it resembled
no vinaigrette ever seen in France. As nobody since
the time of the emperor Charlemagne had made a salad
except with greens, dressed with a little oil, lemon juice,
and salt, the effect was revelatory.

To complete his triumph, Dayan renamed the sacred
Big Mac, calling it the Royal Cheese. By 1976, to the cha-
grin of the home company, he had fourteen restaurants
and was coining money. After repeated attempts to buy
him out, McDonald's sued, claiming he had breached
the rule that a customer passing under the golden arches
anywhere in the world would find a product identical
to the one he ate back home. "Dayan cooked his hamburger patties 180 degrees too high," charged the company. "French fries 50 degrees too high; fish 55 degrees
too high; and apple pie 67 degrees too high." As well,
they accused him of bad sanitation. Obviously unaware
of the leisurely behavior of French waiters, they also
complained that "customers waited for service for more
than three minutes!"

McDonald's won. Dayan relinquished the franchise
and changed the name of his chain to O'Kitch. It was

swiftly swallowed up by his rivals. But Ronald McDonald had learned his lesson. Today, although the exter-
nal trappings may be the same all over the world, the
product is customized to fit often inexplicable local taste.
Businesses flourish and fail, lawsuits are lost or won, but
meat goes on.

Beef had to feature somewhere in my imaginary
banquet, but its very popularity caused problems.
No beef dish was truly uncommon, so there was nothing new to discover. The grilled entrecôte, or faux filet,
was a cliché of lunch menus, and for dinner, larger places
usually featured, as a dish for two, the piece of filet
known as a Chateaubriand and the classic *côte de boeuf*,
or rib roast. Once you got into boiled or braised beef,
you could take your pick from among a dozen dishes:
boeuf bourguignon, boeuf en daube, pot-au-feu . . .

Then Marie-Dominique asked, "What about a tartare?"

"A tartare of what?"

Lately, the term had been stretched to include
chopped raw tuna, salmon, even tomato. A Japanese restaurant in New York served what one reviewer called "a
so-called tartare, consisting of edamame [soybean pods]

chopped with shiso [an herb] and citrus." But Marie-Dominique, like any good Frenchwoman, scorned such perversions.

"*Boeuf, naturalement.*"

Nothing brings meat eaters closer to the pure enjoyment of flesh than the classic steak tartare. This is beef naked, raw, and unashamed. A piece of lean steak is chopped finely—ideally with two sharp knives—given a minimum of seasoning, and served with, at most, a little salad and a few frites.

Or at least that's how it should be.

Unfortunately, the average restaurant buys its tartare prechopped in vacuum-packed single servings of about 200 grams, or half a pound. Others use fresh meat but mince it, a process that, if you believe the experts, tears the beef, stretching and tangling its fibers. Everyone agrees that the worst option is the food processor. Beef that's been through a *robot*, as the French call a processor, emerges as a pink paste, juiceless, bland, and inedible.

Even restaurants that respect tartare feel a need to improve it. They bring the meat to you as a patty, surrounded by small heaps of chopped onion, parsley, pickled cucumber, and capers, with a raw egg yolk squatting on top. The waiter asks if you wish it *préparée*—prepared.

If you do, he disappears, to return with all the additions mixed in, and carrying bottles of Worcestershire sauce, mustard, ketchup, and Tabasco, in case you feel it needs even more.

M. F. K. Fisher, while agreeing the dish was "slightly barbaric" and that many Americans would find it inedible, stood up for the pure and unadulterated tartare. The chopped beef, in her opinion, should contain no more than fresh herbs, an egg yolk, salt, pepper, and a little olive oil. "Keep it from the eager exhibitionism of the waiter," she urged—still good advice.

I'd never thought of including a tartare in my feast. Like all those other beef dishes, it was too familiar. But I really knew nothing about it. In what region had it developed? Was it even traditional? Did Rabelais sit down to a tartare? Did Toulouse-Lautrec?

"I might consider it, I suppose. Why?"

Marie-Dominique plunked down the week's *Nouvelle Observateur*, open at the restaurant page.

"Because this establishment is supposed to be"—she read over my shoulder—" 'the nirvana of tartare.' "

If you're used to the chilly, knowing tone of *The New Yorker*'s restaurant reviews, French food writing can startle with its undisguised greed. This notice throbbed with appetite.

Imagine this tartare. A hefty serving of 350 grams ("We do not weigh it, monsieur!"), prepared with delicacy and elegance, which is to say finely but not copiously seasoned, with whole capers in sufficiently small numbers to avoid acidity. This is the art of seasoning; to avoid the "big guns" but add it by the millimeter and leave the meat enough time to recover. It arrives accompanied by frites to die for—large, irregular, crunchy, and melting at the same time—and a salad of young greens, fresh and peppery, with nothing but a little oil. And the chopping? I know what you think, purists of the steak tartare. I see you already climbing onto the cooking pot and raising your forks to heaven; "It's not a real tartare unless you chop it with knives!" You're wrong. Pleasure and taste can hide anywhere, and here, believe me, they jump in your face, knives or no knives.

"It does sound interesting," I conceded.

"So I thought." Marie-Dominique looked at the clock. "I believe today you are taking me to lunch."

•　　•　　•

Why are the best restaurants always the hardest to find? Some lurk behind unmarked doors, in obscure streets where, in normal circumstances, you wouldn't go unarmed. Many don't take reservations or, if they do, impose them with a strictness worthy of a house of detention. Ma Maison, once the most fashionable eating place in Los Angeles, didn't list its telephone number. Hours of opening vary perversely for such establishments. They shut their doors without notice for a month of renovations, or take a week's holiday to attend some family celebration, or for even more improbable reasons. (This isn't confined to restaurants. When our daughter was about to be born, the clinic rejected our suggested date. "It's the start of the ski season," explained the receptionist. When I asked, "Does that matter?," she said, straight-faced, "Only if you don't want your child delivered by the gardener.")

The reviewer didn't exaggerate when he described the location of the tartare restaurant as "a little lost corner of the *quatorzième*." Though the fourteenth arrondissement boasts the great cafés of Montparnasse, La Coupole, La Dôme, La Rotonde, and Le Select, it's dominated by the cemetery, the sprawl of the railway terminus, and the looming black horror of Paris's only skyscraper, the Tour de Montparnasse. Surrounding them is a maze of narrow one-way streets that can have you chasing your tail for hours.

Normally, one wouldn't have looked at the restaurant twice. Small and modern, it occupied a shop front on a corner of an otherwise unremarkable street. But inside, all sense of the present evaporated. Despite some updating, it still retained an original terrazzo floor and the custom of chalking up the menu on a board. The dishes, too, were classic: *boudin noir*, *blanquette*, fish soup . . . and steak tartare.

Certain words signify an establishment that respects traditional dishes and methods. *Maison* is one. It means something has been made "in house" and is likely a specialty of the chef. *Artisanal* signifies something created by hand, not in a factory. And *à l'ancienne* means it's in the old style, just the way mother or—even better—grandmother used to make it.

This place delivered all three. The bread wasn't the ubiquitous sliced baguette but chunks of Poilâne's wholemeal sourdough, solid and elastic, with a crust that fought your teeth. The house wine came in a clear glass bottle with a heavy base, the kind you see in movies from the 1930s, where one thug is usually smashing it over the head of another.

Our tartares arrived *préparées*, with salad and *frites* all on the same plate. I tried a *frite*. Thick-cut, well browned but not crisp, it was happily remote from the shriveled slivers served at burger joints.

The tartare itself was just as uncompromising. In my first forkful, I tasted finely chopped onion and whole capers, but aside from the egg yolk, salt, and pepper, nothing else. The satisfaction of pure beef was unimpaired. Everything was *comme il faut*—the way it should be.

The review had promised that the restaurant's tartare would "tickle our carnivore pleasure." It did that. But where was the rarity that would justify including it in my banquet? Perhaps, in some remote corner of the country, there existed a variation that no longer appeared in Paris restaurants, but I had no idea what it could be. In fact, my ignorance of the tartare was profound.

I began my research on the Internet. One site claimed the dish got its name from the Tatars, who invaded Europe in the fourteenth and fifteenth centuries. Supposedly they gnawed raw meat as they rode, too busy looting and pillaging to stop and cook. Another authority agreed Tatars were mixed up in it somewhere but suggested that warriors put meat under their saddle in the morning so that the pounding of the day's riding, plus the effect of the animal's sweat, would tenderize it by nightfall. I didn't care to think how this made it taste, but it called to mind another favorite of these people, a drink called *kumis*, made from fermented mare's milk. I once met a man who'd drunk it. What was it like? "Well," he said. "At first, it's like thin yogurt. Then you get this alcoholic rush—and, immediately after, an awful aftertaste of horseshit."

A third theory claimed tartare got its name because it was originally served with sauce tartare, made from mayonnaise mixed with chopped onion, capers, and pickles. This surprised me. Sauce tartare usually accompanies fish, not meat. But was it just coincidence that sauce tartare and steak tartare shared some ingredients: pickles, capers, onion?

I dug further, looking for the ur-recipe that marked the birthplace of this icon of French cuisine. It didn't take long. The dish appeared for the first time in the 1921 edition of Escoffier's *Le Guide Culinaire*. Back then it wasn't called steak tartare but *steak à l'Americaine*—steak American-style.

It soon became clear that I had stumbled on a great secret. Forget those stories about Tatar warriors. Steak tartare came to France with entirely different foreign invaders: the Yanks who flooded into Paris in 1917 as soldiers and returned a few years later as tourists. Steak tartare was just a burger and fries, with the ingredients rearranged to suit French taste.

I could almost reconstruct the moment of invention: 1919. Two Americans in a Montparnasse bistro, probably drunk, are trying to explain to a waiter that they want a hamburger—something which, although it was invented in Chicago in 1904, was totally unknown everywhere else. They probably described the ingredients—minced beef, with onion and a pickle—and were astonished when he returned with all these, just differently arranged.

"No, no, we said rare, not raw . . ."

And meanwhile, in the kitchen, the chef is tasting it and saying, "Y'know, these Americans are crazy, but this isn't half bad . . ."

As I was musing on this, Marie-Dominique materialized behind me.

"So . . . are you going to include a tartare in your feast?"

I slammed the Escoffier shut.

"Er . . . haven't decided."

But I had, really. There would be no tartare at my table. If it ever got around that I'd exposed this French classic as an American invention, what restaurant would ever serve me again?

Fifteen

First Catch Your Hare

*Hare à la Royale at Montparnasse, roast piglet at the
Odéon, comfits in the Saint-Michel square . . . Such dishes
may not be exclusive to the Left Bank, but here they had
their origin and can be savored in surroundings conducive to
indolent enjoyment.*

Paris Rive Gauche, Official Guide of the Chamber
of Commerce of the Left Bank of Paris, 1957/58

Occasionally, heading out of Paris to a far corner
of France, I wondered if I was neglecting my
home city. Shouldn't any banquet taking place in Paris
include at least one dish that was unique to Paris?

Immediately a problem presented itself. There aren't
any.

When I ate lampreys in Bergerac, bouillabaisse in
Sète, *moules* in Fouras, or *socca* in Antibes, I had been,
in the fashionable term, a locavore. The ingredients had
come from within a few kilometers of, if not from, the
actual neighborhood.

But nobody grew much in Paris anymore.

In 1780, 1,600 varieties of fruit, flower, and plant were found in the Paris area, including 104 types of fungi. Individual villages on the outskirts were famous for their produce: Argenteuil for asparagus, Montreuil for peaches, Montmorency for cherries, Vaugirard for strawberries, Saint-Germain for peas, Clamart for artichokes. Each morning, in season, supplies of all these arrived at Les Halles, making it possible to prepare dishes with a distinctive local character.

Cherry picking at Montmorency

Those orchards and farms are gone, engulfed by apartment buildings and autoroutes. In Britain, local councils divide waste ground into allotments where people can cultivate their own vegetables. This has kept alive a tradition of home-grown produce. But Paris has no such program. A few tiny vineyards survive in Montmartre, Belleville, and in what used to be Vaugirard, where, significantly, the vines are part of a park for children. Any examples of cultivation are as exotic as camels or polar bears to modern Parisians, who bring their children on Sunday afternoons to stare and wonder.

Admittedly, white button mushrooms were called *champignons de Paris* and ordinary boiled ham *jambon de Paris*, but neither was particularly Parisian. Escoffier listed a few dishes as *à la Parisienne*, including a rice pilaf with chicken, but since his recipes for *pilaf à la Grecque* . . . *Orientale*, and . . . *Turque* used the same ingredients, give or take a pinch of saffron, powdered ginger, or a few raisins, the label hardly seemed earned.

In her *French Regional Cooking*, Anne Willan suggests potage St. Germain and *canard* Montmorency as Paris specialties. The potage, a soup containing green peas and shredded lettuce, might have begun life in the fields of the Abbey of Saint-Germain-des-Pré, which once occupied a large portion of the Left Bank, but peas and lettuce grow everywhere, and it could just as easily have been invented in Lyon or Lille. *Canard* Montmorency, a dish of duck breast, used the sour cherries for which Montmorency used to be famous, but the village was fifteen kilometers outside the city, and so hardly Parisian. In an early version of pick-your-own, people would travel there on weekends, hire a cherry tree for the day, and pig out. Ironically, not a single cherry tree remains there.

As for *Lievre à la Royale*, the hare dish that the Left Bank Chamber of Commerce suggested was everyday eating in Montparnasse, I suspect this was a practical joke, on a level with sending the new apprentice to buy a can of striped paint or a left-handed screwdriver.

Cooking hare is a tortuous business, starting with securing the animal itself. When Isabella Beeton published her *Book of Household Management* in 1861, she wisely began her recipe for Jugged Hare, "First catch your hare." This is good advice. The hare is wily, agile, and may be killed only in season. Since its blood plays an important part in the cooking, it can't be bought already butchered but must be shot with precision or, more often, snared, and the blood drained while still fresh. At the end of the nineteenth century, hunters were known to travel as far as 120 miles to the fields around Tours and spend a week finding a prime specimen.

Once the hare had hung long enough for the meat to rot into a suitable state of gaminess, the cook could get to work. Jointing the animal, he sautéed the pieces in goose fat and bacon, then braised them in two bottles of red wine, with twenty cloves of garlic and forty shallots—so finely chopped, dictated the standard recipe, "as to attain as near as possible an almost molecular state." Once the meat was sufficiently tender that it needed only a spoon to eat it, the blood, along with two glasses of cognac, was mixed into the cooking juices to create the sauce. Not a dish likely to turn up on the menu of a mom-and-pop café in Bohemian Montparnasse.

Just as I was about to abandon hope of finding a uniquely Parisian dish, a casual aside by Anne Willan caught my eye: "The onion soup and grilled pig's feet of the brasseries of Les Halles," she wrote, "have become an institution."

Of course! What was I thinking of? What dishes were more typical of Paris than these? I'd dallied with pigs' feet in the past and never found their cooking worth the tiny amount of gelatinous meat they yielded. But *soupe à l'oignon* was classic, a dish not only of culinary importance but one with a role in the cultural, artistic, and literary traditions of the nation. And it was specifically and typically Parisian—even wedded to a precise district: the streets around the old produce market of Les Halles.

So far, I hadn't tried cooking any of the dishes I'd imagined for my *repas*, but now I was inspired. I would make my own onion soup.

Yes, I was that dumb.

Sixteen

First Catch Your Bouillon

Beautiful soup! Who cares for fish, game or any other dish? Who would not give all else for two pennyworth of beautiful soup?

Lewis Carroll, *Alice's Adventures in Wonderland*

One should never eat soup on Sunday. Not in a Paris restaurant, anyway.

In fact, try not to eat out on Sunday in Paris at all.

Markets shut at noon on Sunday and don't reopen until Tuesday morning. Most small restaurants also close. If larger places remain open, it's seldom with a chef in attendance—just a skeleton staff and a menu of dishes prepared ahead of time, ready for the microwave.

That's not a problem with *boeuf bourguignon* or cassoulet, which can taste even better a day or two after they're made. But fishing boats don't put to sea on weekends, so your *sole meunière* will have last seen the ocean three days before—something all the butter and lemon

juice in the world can't disguise. As for oysters, the man who opens them also takes the weekend off, leaving a few dozen in the refrigerator. By the time they reach you, they'll be shriveled, dry, and gamy.

And let's not even think about desserts: *Crème brûlée*, its sugar crust sticky after days in the fridge, *île flottante* with the *crème anglaise* developing that nasty custard skin, and a *gâteau chocolat* of stale cake layered with cream gone hard as butter in the fridge.

Even against these odds, however, I wouldn't have thought one could make a mess of onion soup.

One minute we were sitting with our feet up, enjoying our Sunday morning croissants and coffee, and contemplating a leisurely visit to a *brocante*. An hour later we were organizing a birthday dinner for fourteen on behalf of some friends who'd just flown in from New York on the spur of the moment and wanted to celebrate an anniversary. We don't even own fourteen chairs, so squeezing everyone around our dining table wasn't an option. Also, because the new arrivals were starry-eyed about "traditional Paris restaurants," we decided, foolishly, to eat out.

The few smaller establishments that did open on Sunday couldn't manage such a large party, so we compromised on a place known for period design rather than good food. The visitors loved its art nouveau décor, with the polished brass and varnished wood paneling. But we should have been warned by the many empty tables and the waiters loitering at the rear. Sunday evening was, for them and for the restaurant, the low point of the week. They looked as displeased with our invasion as with that of the Nazis in 1940.

Rather than taking orders for aperitifs, our waiter simply inquired, "Champagne for everyone?," and turned to go. He was visibly annoyed when we called him back. With no barman on duty, he had to mix the drinks himself. His Kirs were 99 percent wine with only a dash of syrup, and he interpreted "dry martini" as Martini Bianco on the rocks.

Meanwhile, we contemplated the menus. Bound in grease-spotted red velour, they were long on illustrations of cancan girls and gentlemen in handlebar mustaches, but short on actual food. I recognized the old standbys: *salades composées*, *soupe au poisson*, *soupe à l'oignon*, and a *soupe du jour*. Then *confit de canard*, *boeuf bourguignon*, *coq au vin*—surely all canned or boil-in-the-bag.

When I asked about the *soupe du jour*, the waiter disappeared for five minutes, to return with the news, not unexpected, that it was *potage printanier*. Supposedly made from spring vegetables, this is the gentile version of Jewish carrot soup: in Yiddish, *tzimmes*. To make a new dish, runs kitchen wisdom, just combine all your leftovers, heat, and stir well. *Tzimmes* embodies this rule so perfectly that the word also describes any deal tossed together with too many variables and not enough forethought. "A prolonged procedure," says one definition, " an involved business; trouble."

In 1962, Eugène Ionesco contributed a script to a movie called *The Seven Deadly Sins*. He chose to illustrate "anger" through the medium of *potage printanier*. All over France, husbands lose their temper at yet again being served the same soup for Sunday lunch, and, moreover, finding a fly in it. Thousands of domestic arguments escalate into nuclear war and the end of the world. Nobody in France thought this was extreme. Many were surprised it hadn't happened already.

O n that Sunday night, Marie-Dominique and a few others ordered *soupe à l'oignon*. It seemed a safe, if cliché, choice. One just ladled onion broth into a bowl, floated a piece of toast on top, sprinkled grated Gruyère, and browned it under the grill. What could go wrong?

The soups arrived with their cheese almost bubbling yet not brown—a sure sign they were only seconds out of the microwave. Marie-Dominique poked hers with her spoon. The yellow surface resisted like plastic. And when she lifted the spoon, the cheese came with it, stuck to the spoon as if with Krazy Glue. So did a slab of sodden bread as thick as a hamburger bun. Underneath, where there should have been soup, the bowl was almost dry. Sitting in the fridge for so long, the liquid had been completely soaked up by the bread.

She called after the departing waiter, *"M'sieur, s'il vous plait*, where is my soup?"

He swung back to the table. "Zis is your soup, madame," he said loftily in English. "*Soupe à l'oignon Française.* Is in zer French style."

Trying to pass off a dud dish as "the way it's served in France"? To a Frenchwoman, and a Parisienne at that? And with as sacred a dish as *soupe à l'oignon*? He should have cut his throat right then.

O ver the centuries, soup in France has accumulated a body of myth, tradition, and lore. One speaks of it in the same respectful, capitalized way as The Nation, The Heavens, The Earth. It's not "soup" but *La Soupe*: symbolic, metaphoric, sacramental.

The respect is understandable. Mankind emerged from an oceanic soup. As babies, we grow in an amniotic soup within our mother's bodies, and once born, we are fed on soup. Soup sustains and consoles the destitute, the ill, the desperate. It has entered the language at every level. To indicate that dinner's ready, we say "Soup's on!," while to give universal offense one "spits in the soup." At its best, soup is warmth, reassurance, sustenance. Soup is Home. It is Faith, Hope, and Charity. It may even be God.

At the core of soup is broth, the essence of meat, vegetables, and spices, suffused through water, which the French call bouillon. For centuries, the French, Italians, Portuguese, and British have regarded it as both food and medicine. The word *restaurant* derives from an innkeeper in the 1700s who offered soup in order to *restaurer*, or restore, his clients. In 1750, John Huxham's *An Essay on Fevers* recommended chicken broth to rebalance the "humors."

As he traveled through France in 1765, the English novelist Tobias Smollett, suffering from tuberculosis, was constantly offered bouillon, though he doubted it did him any good.

> *Bouillon is a universal remedy among the good*
> *people of France; insomuch, that they have no idea*
> *of any person's dying, after having swallowed un*
> *bon bouillon. One of the English gentlemen who*
> *were robbed and murdered about thirty years ago*
> *between Calais and Boulogne, being brought to*
> *the post-house of Boulogne with some signs of life,*
> *this remedy was immediately administered. "What*
> *surprises me greatly," said the post-master, "I made*
> *an excellent bouillon, and poured it down his throat*
> *with my own hands, and yet he did not recover."*

Sometimes, though, broth worked wonders. In 1672, in Saint-Didier, near Avignon, the crowd halted the hanging of one Pierre du Fort when the public executioner bungled the job. After seeing the hangman and his girlfriend swinging on the hapless Pierre's legs in the hope of strangling him, the spectators decided he'd suffered enough. They cut him down and carried him to a monastery, where he was given wine and "each Saturday, bouillon made with meat," a treatment on which he made a full recovery, presumably to rob and murder again.

Every country has a different way of losing its temper in a restaurant. Britons and Americans shout, pound the table, fling down napkins, and demand to See the Manager. Think of Jack Nicholson raging at a waitress about a chicken salad sandwich in the film *Five Easy Pieces*. Chinese and Japanese sit silent, with bowed heads, waiting for the offender to acknowledge his error and make amends. Italians have been known to weep and Spaniards to challenge waiters to a fight. Germans, coldly rational, collect names, writing them in their *Persönliches gastronomisches schwarzbuch*, or personal gastronomic black book, a small diary kept exclusively for this purpose, I'm told.

The French insult. Reflecting the fact that France is still at heart rural, its slang contains numerous references to animals and plants, ideal for berating restaurant staff. *Vache* (cow) predominates. "*La vache!*" expresses anger or dismay. Symbols of stupidity include *cornichon* (pickle), *citrouille* (pumpkin), and *navet* (turnip). Each gains force when prefixed by "*Espèce d'une . . .*"—"a prime example of . . ."

It was bad luck for the waiter that day that one of our French friends, Jean-Marc, was a master of invective. In an insistently menacing tone, he began by suggesting the man resembled the *andouille*—a sausage made of pigs' intestines, including the rectum. He went on to compare him to a root vegetable customarily fed to livestock, and was just rolling out one of his favorites—"*Vous avez le cerveau d'une baguette fromage*" ("You have the brain of a cheese sandwich")—when the manager, summoned from his comfortable office where he was probably watching the football replay on TV, arrived to calm things down.

"You have the brains of a moldy rutabaga!"

Recognizing a disaster in the making, he distributed champagne and foie gras to all and tore up our bill. We last saw our waiter slinking out the door in street clothes, having been sent home early, if not actually fired. He was lucky. Men have been strung up from lampposts for lesser sins than interfering with onion soup.

Once I thought of cooking *soupe à l'oignon*, the idea took hold. Of course, onion soup was far too robust to begin a dinner of the kind I visualized. It was a meal in itself. The bouillon at the start of a great meal should be, at most, a consommé—light, thin, transparent, stimulating the appetite rather than satisfying it. But since a bowl of asparagus soup had suggested the idea for the banquet, to prepare *soupe à la oignon* embodied a certain poetic rightness.

All the same, I discussed it with Boris first.

He proposed we meet in a restaurant I'd never heard of, called Le Mine au Poivre—The Pepper Mine. It was on rue Montcalm, in the eighteenth, one of the narrow streets that run downhill from the walled sprawl of the Cimetière Montmartre.

Some people visit the cemetery to lay flowers on the tomb of their aunt, but most are tourists, seeking its many celebrity graves: that of Nijinsky, with its morose statue of the dancer slumped in his *Petrushka* costume; of Adolphe Sax, inventor of the saxophone, the only tomb in the world decorated with a facsimile of that instrument; or the resting place of Marie Duplessis, original Lady of the Camellias, inspiration of *Camille* and of Violetta in *La Traviata*. As she died young and destitute, a lover paid for her tomb in a sheltered spot in the lee of low wall. The sun falls lightly on her sandstone crypt, which, in the season, is often decorated with fresh camellias.

Like a gated community of the prosperous departed, the cemetery has only one entrance, and that on the uphill side. Most days, the streets around contain a steady flow of hot and exasperated tourists and mourners who, having got off the bus at the downhill end, must trudge around the entire circumference to get in.

Because of this, nearby streets are well supplied with bars into which parched and weary strangers can retreat for a reviving beer. Le Mine au Poivre was just such a place: a shady retreat to escape from the heat, catch your breath, enjoy a drink, and maybe a snack.

I might have walked right past except for the music drifting out its door—an old Tina Turner number, but sung in French. Glancing in, I saw Boris at the back, near the door to the kitchen. Above him, a large painted board announced "Vérigood."

"*Vérigood?*" I said as I sat down.

He didn't look up. "Jean-Christophe is a bit unconventional."

Confirming this, the music tape segued from "Nutbush City Limits" to the Flower Duet from *Lakmé*.

In these tiny establishments, it's easy to feel one has stepped into a film from the 1940s, one of those dramas about a middle-aged train driver or cinema projectionist driven to murder by his love for a randy and restless woman. *Manon Lescaut* meets *La Bête Humaine*.

The clients here were perfect casting. Who was the killer? Probably the middle-aged man sitting in silence at one of the tables on the sidewalk. And his victim? Obviously the woman opposite him. Clearly their marriage was as flat as the half-drunk glasses of Stella Artois on the table between them.

At the bar, a tall man paged through the left-wing daily *Liberation*. In the film, he would be the world-weary cop who solves the case. Two stools along, a thin woman of what the French call "a certain age," with a mass of black frizzy hair, drank a dusky glass of Pernod, and offered her bony profile to be admired. Too old and severe for the femme fatale, she could be the malicious neighbor forced by a shady past to inform on the killer.

"What can I bring you, m'sieur?"

The man I'd last noticed reading *Liberation* was now standing by our table, holding a bottle of wine.

"Meet Jean-Christophe," Boris said. "This is his place."

We shook hands. I pointed to the sign.

"Why 'Vérigood.'"

"Because *is* very good."

"What is?"

"His *boeuf bourguignon*," Boris said.

"Best in Paris," said Jean-Christophe. "Fifteen hours the cooking."

He poured half a glass of red for Boris and looked at me.

"He's Australian," Boris said.

"Ah!" He topped up my glass, looked at the bottle, still half full, and left it on the table. "Then I bring another," he said. "Or maybe two?"

The music tape switched to a reedy, wailing tenor, singing in what sounded like Arabic.

"How *is* the beef?" I asked Boris when he'd gone

He shrugged. "I like it. Make up your own mind."

It reminded me why I was here. "I told you I was thinking of doing *soupe à l'oignon*?"

"Brave man."

"Why? How hard can it be? Every café serves *soupe à l'oignon*. I've even done it with a stock cube."

Without turning his head, Boris said, "Jean-Christophe, do you have a beef stock cube?"

Jean-Christophe's head emerged from below the bar, where he was sorting bottles.

"Why I would want such a thing?"

"Find one, could you?"

To my surprise, he came round the bar, walked out the front door, and crossed the road to the little market opposite.

Boris asked, "Do you remember how Giotto proved his mastery?"

"Something about a circle?"

"Yes. When the Pope asked for proof of his skill, he just took a brush and drew a perfect circle, freehand."

"And cooking *soupe à l'oignon* is the perfect circle?"

"Some might say so. Close, anyway. Do you have a *Guide Culinaire*?"

"The Escoffier? You know I do. A first edition. Inscribed."

"But have you read it?"

"Nobody *reads* Escoffier. It's like a Windows manual. I've *consulted* it."

Published in 1903, *Le Guide Culinaire* of Georges-Auguste Escoffier has never been out of print. Its eight hundred closely printed pages summarize the wealth of French cuisine, but also its complexity. If you want to know how to skin, cook, and remove the meat from a calf's head, purée a sea urchin, make *cailles* (quail) *Richelieu*, cook red cabbage in the Flemish style, or prepare a jellied dessert called My Queen, it will tell you—though in a quirky and obtuse manner that's peculiarly Escoffier and uniquely French.

Jean-Christophe returned and dropped an orange-and-yellow box on the table.

"Bouillon gout BOEUF" was lettered on it in yellow, next to a cartoon of a bull. Below were photos of a large brown onion and a bunch of fresh herbs, both beaded with morning dew. The words *riche en gout*—rich in flavor—ran vertically down the pack.

"Read the ingredients," Boris said. "If you can find them."

The list appeared in minuscule lettering on the end of the pack.

" 'Salt,' " I read. " 'Malt extract; flavor extenders; sodium glutamate, guynamate, and inosanate; sunflower oil; corn-based flavorings, including beef, sugar, onion, parsley; extracts of pepper, clove, celery, bay, and thyme; caramel (sugar and water); vegetable fibers. May contain traces of milk and egg.' "

"Notice that there's no actual beef," Boris said. "It doesn't even promise beef—just the taste of beef. And it fails even to deliver that." He snorted. "Read Escoffier. Chapter one, page one. Then we can talk."

Before I left, I tried Jean-Christophe's *boeuf bourguignon*. Instead of the usual stringy meat swimming in watery gravy, with boiled potatoes and carrots, it arrived in a dark heap, barely moist, with no accompaniment beyond a bed of homemade mashed potatoes. The meat fell apart under the fork, tender and succulent. In a word, *vérigood*. Fifteen hours of cooking hadn't been wasted.

In his oblique way, Boris was giving me a lesson. Good cooking permits no short cuts. To be worthy of creating, even in imagination, a truly great meal, I must prove myself competent in the skills of the master cook. I would never be Escoffier, but I could aspire to be a menial sous chef, the most junior member of the *brigade de cuisine*, the apprentice charged with the dull but crucial task of preparing *bouillon*. Having achieved that goal, he might consider me worthy to move on to greater things—even to the roasting of that elusive ox.

Seventeen

First Catch Your Chef

A very strong will, sustained by a glass of excellent champagne.
Sarah Bernhardt's formula for "unfailing vitality,"
as confided to Georges-Auguste Escoffier

The French like a little rogue in their cultural heroes, so it was predictable that Georges-Auguste Escoffier, who transformed the art of cooking, should be a thief and embezzler, just like his friend and partner, the hotelier César Ritz.

Ritz, cold-eyed and expressionless, with a nattily waxed black mustache, had a face that belonged on a "Wanted" poster. But Escoffier embodied that most flattering of adjectives: *suave*. His silver hair and mustache, his impeccable suits, his gleaming shoes with their built-up heels and discreet elevator insoles to increase his height, combined in a vision of sleek and peerless probity.

Georges-Auguste Escoffier

In 1888, Richard D'Oyly Carte, the entrepreneur who used the profits from producing Gilbert and Sullivan's comic operas to build the Savoy Hotel on London's Strand, invited Ritz to become its manager and Escoffier the *chef de cuisine*. Leading what they called "a little army of hotel men," the two invaded England.

London's gourmets soon learned that the Savoy could offer dishes not available anywhere else. Escoffier imported *ortolans* and truffles from France, golden Sterlet caviar from Russia, and would send word to a favored client when the first asparagus of the season arrived from Provence. It soon became fashionable among society families to give their household servants a night off once a week and hold a dinner party in the Savoy's lofty dining room and grill, overlooking the Thames.

Like Vatel and many others before him, Escoffier recognized the value of showmanship. He staged dinners to order, often on themes proposed by the host. American food writer Julian Street explained the right way to go about dining out.

> *One should go in advance to the restaurant of one's*
> *choice, consult the proprietor or the head waiter,*
> *select one's dishes, and then obtain the advice of*
> *the wine waiter . . . Never ask members of your*
> *party to order for themselves. A scattering of varied*
> *orders disorganizes the kitchen and the service,*
> *and destroys the suavity of the meal. Let the same*
> *courses be served to all, as you would if you were*
> *entertaining in your own home.*

To clients who paid him this compliment, Escoffier gave good value. For a woman's birthday, he created a menu in which the first letters of the dishes spelled out her name, Marguerite: M*ousseline au Crevettes Roses,* A*mourettes au Consommé,* R*ougets en Papillotes . . .* Asked for an exceptional dish, he dreamed up Nymphs in the

Dawn: frogs' legs tinted pink and embedded with fresh
tarragon and chervil in clear champagne jelly to suggest
river sprites hiding among water plants.

His signature color was pink. Many of his dishes were
colored and flavored with dark red Rozen paprika from
Hungary, which used only the outer flesh and skin of the
pepper. He would have been the perfect chef to orchestrate
one of the dinners held by the notorious Paris courtesan
Cora Pearl. After dancing nude on orchids, she had herself
served up on an enormous platter as the main dish, nestling
on flowers and wearing nothing but a pink sauce.

This was a little too louche for Escoffier, but in October 1895 he did agree to a special request that let him
run riot with red food.

A group of young English gamblers had won 350,000
francs at Monte Carlo by betting on red and the number
nine at roulette. Regulars at the Savoy, they asked Escoffier to stage a dinner celebrating their luck.

*Everything was red and gold. The table was
decorated with petals of red roses. The menus were
red. The chairs were red, and had the lucky winning
number 9 stuck on them. The banquet room was
decorated with palm trees to evoke the Riviera, and
these were strung with red light bulbs.*

Only red wine was served, and every one of the nine courses featured at least one red dish. Red smoked salmon with caviar was followed by red snapper, lamb cooked pink, with tomatoes and red beans, a chicken with red lettuce salad, asparagus in a pink sauce called *Coucher de Soleil sur un Beau Soir d'Été* (Sunset on a Beautiful Summer Evening), foie gras in a paprika-colored jelly, concluding with an ice sculpture of the mountain behind Monte Carlo, lit with red lights, and with a nest of red autumn leaves supporting a bowl of *mousse de Curacao* covered in strawberries.

Escoffier loved to show off, particularly to celebrities. He designed two dishes for the Australian-born opera diva Nellie Melba. Nervously preoccupied with her throat, she feared ordinary toast might scratch it, while ice cream, her favorite dessert, could chill her vocal cords. He ordered slices of toast cut in half horizontally, then re-toasted, to make ultra-thin Melba Toast, and invented a dish of fresh peaches on vanilla ice cream, coated in raspberry purée, which he called Peach Melba.

While he was chef at the Grand Hotel in Monte Carlo, the soprano Adelina Patti often stayed there. A Swiss couple named Jungbluth owned the Grand, and when Patti, perhaps overwhelmed by the richness of

Escoffier's menus, asked what he cooked for the Jung-bluths, they invited her to lunch.

Escoffier had planned a simple Alsatian *pot-au-feu* of boiled beef and salt pork with carrots, potatoes, and cabbage. But his pride wouldn't allow him to present anything so everyday to the great Patti. "In view of the occasion," he wrote, "I thought I would be forgiven for expanding on this 'simple family meal.'"

Lunch began with the *pot-au-feu* served tradition-ally, starting with a soup made from the broth, followed by the meat and vegetables, with horseradish sauce. After that, however, he pulled out all the stops.

> *I served an excellent Bresse chicken that I threaded with strips of pork fat and roasted on an open spit, and also a mixed salad of chicory leaves and beets. Next, a magnificent parfait de foie gras appeared on the table, made up of a mixture of Alsatian foie gras and Périgord truffles. I completed this exceptional family meal with an orange mousse surrounded by strawberries macerated in Curacao.*

After that, the soprano might have felt she needed to cut down on eating, but there Escoffier was no help. To one hostess who fretted about her weight, he proposed a

"Diet Dinner": caviar, shrimp, oysters, turtle soup, sole, trout, a champagne sorbet, asparagus, ending with a paprika soufflé and pears in port.

Though César Ritz managed the Savoy until 1897, he was seldom there. Instead, he buzzed around Europe and the Mediterranean, consulting for other hotels and supervising the new Ritz, then being built on Place Vendôme in Paris. "When in London you are hardly ever in the hotel except to eat and sleep," complained the Savoy owners. "You have latterly been simply using The Savoy as a place to live in, a pied-à-terre, an office, from which to carry on your other schemes and as a lever to float a number of other projects in which the Savoy has no interest whatever."

Plentiful graft was already built into the hotel system. In addition to the usual bribes from grocers, butchers, and linen laundries, champagne companies kicked back a small sum for every cork that proved a bottle had been drunk. Not content, Escoffier and Ritz had started the Ritz Hotel Development Company, which sold supplies to the Savoy at inflated prices.

When the hotel audited the accounts, Ritz couldn't explain what had become of £11,000 in wine—worth twenty times that sum in today's money. It was probably diverted, via the Ritz Hotel Development Company, to the cellars of the new Paris hotel. Escoffier also agreed he owed the Savoy £8,000 but claimed he could only pay £500, the rest presumably having been spirited across the Channel. In March 1897 he and Ritz were dismissed, along with their supply manager and kitchen staff. At first, the sixteen cooks refused to leave and resisted with carving knives until the police arrived to march them out. Escoffier managed to blame the scandal on British obtuseness.

We had saved the Savoy from bankruptcy, brought it to the summit of glory, and given its shareholders the satisfaction they merited. It would have been possible for these gentlemen to solve their differences in everyone's interest and without anyone losing face. They would have none of it.

Once the Ritz opened in Paris, the Ritz Hotel Development Company switched to recruiting kitchen staff for other hotels and handling supplies. The partners also had their revenge on the Savoy when the owners of London's new Carlton Hotel hired them to run it. Known as the Ritz-Carlton, their new venture creamed off most of the Savoy's society business.

All this unpleasantness didn't mar Escoffier's legend. Rather, it became part of it. "Don't let his manners fool you," murmured people on the inside. "The old fox is smarter than he looks. He really put it over those *rosbifs*."

Few people have influenced the way we eat more than Escoffier. During the 1870 Franco-Prussian War, he was called up as part of the reserve and put in charge of cooking for the officers of the Second Division headquarters at Metz, the most easterly city in France, next to the German border.

Watching the army at work convinced him that his profession could benefit from military discipline. A kitchen should be staffed like an army unit, with a *brigade de cuisine*, commanded by a chief, or *chef*, at the head of a group of professionals chosen for their individual skills: a *saucier* for sauces, a *rôtisseur* for meats, a *patissier* for pastry. After the war, *chef* became the accepted term for a supervisory cook, and the system of kitchen management Escoffier pioneered remains much the same today.

Escoffier insisted on uniform dress in his kitchens: the now-standard white jacket, trousers, and apron, and the high white cap, or toque, to keep sweat and hair out of the food. He also told his staff to trim their hair and shave off their mustaches, but at this, they drew the line. Half his cooks at the Savoy were French and half Italian.

Each regarded a mustache as a sign of status, something that Ritz and Escoffier, both mustachioed, should have understood. Among cooks, a mustache also signified their superiority over waiters and other lower orders, who always shaved. When British writer George Orwell worked as a dishwasher in a Paris hotel during the late 1920s, the *chef du personnel* was scandalized by his facial hair. "*Nom de Dieu!* Who ever heard of a *plongeur* with a mustache?" Orwell had to shave or be fired.

Cooks were also notorious drunks, claiming wine was needed to replace sweat lost at the stove. Escoffier, who never drank or smoked, introduced a healthier substitute: barley water. An energy drink since ancient times—made by boiling grain, straining off the liquid,

Feeding starving soldiers during the Franco-Prussian War, 1870

and flavoring it with lemon—it's still provided to players at tennis tournaments such as Wimbledon. Escoffier placed crocks of it in all his kitchens.

Once in total control of a hotel restaurant and able to employ as many waiters as he needed, he also abandoned *service française*, with a dozen dishes placed on the table at the same time. Instead, he introduced *service à la Russe*, in which each diner simultaneously received an identical dish.

The same rational approach inspired his book *Le Guide Culinaire*. Helped by dozens of chefs, he rounded up details of every dish in French cuisine, arranged them under categories, and described how each should be prepared. With its help, any kitchen could re-create even the most obscure regional specialty.

But the *Guide* is no recipe book. It's a manual. Take, for instance, his entry for a game soup, *Potage Gentilhomme*. Over decades of bad memories and cut corners, it had degenerated into a potato soup with carrots in a chicken bouillon. *Le Guide Culinaire* put it back on track.

Three liters of puree of partridge with lentils, a decaliter of essence of partridge, a decaliter of flaming cognac, the juice of half a lemon, and eight decaliters of high-quality reduced stock made from

*feathered game. For the garnish: little quenelles of
partridge in the form of pearls, and truffles of the
same shape. Two spoonsful to each person.*

A modern recipe book would explain how to make
purée of partridge, game stock, and quenelles, and the
correct way to handle truffles. Escoffier does, but not
in the same chapter and often with even more remote
subsections, variations, and exceptions. He was writing
for professional cooks, who would have learned these
techniques during years of apprenticeship and needed
only reminding. But to the modern cook, accustomed to
convenient, accessible directions and precise measure-
ments, the book is infuriatingly obscure.

American writer Harry Mathews mocked it in his
parody *Country Cooking from Central France: Roast Boned
Rolled Stuffed Shoulder of Lamb (Farce Double)*. Supposedly giving the recipe for "an old French regional dish,"
Mathews concedes that the preparation "demands some
patience, but you will be abundantly rewarded for your
pains." We are then deluged with detail.

*All bones must be removed. If you leave this to the
butcher, have him save them for the deglazing sauce.
The fell or filament must be kept intact, or the*

*flesh may crumble. Set the boned forequarter on the
kitchen table. Do not slice off the purple inspection
stamps but scour them with a brush dipped in a weak
solution of lye. The meat will need all the protection
it can get. Rinse and dry. Marinate the lamb in a
mixture of 2 qts of white wine, 2 qts of olive oil, the
juice of 16 lemons, salt, pepper, 16 crushed garlic
cloves, 10 coarsely chopped yellow onions, basil,
rosemary, melilot, ginger, allspice, and a handful
of juniper berries. The juniper adds a pungent,
authentic note.*

Toward the end, Matthews spares a thought for
the cook. "Do not be upset if you yourself have lost all
desire to eat. This is a normal, salutary condition. Your
satisfaction will have been in the doing, not in the thing
done." Escoffier must often have felt the same way as he
sat down to his own dinner, probably too tired to face
anything more complicated than a boiled egg.

M y own copy of *Le Guide Culinaire* once belonged
to Alexandre Gastaud, chef at New York's Knickerbocker Hotel and later of the Waldorf-Astoria. He'd
worked at the Ritz-Carlton in London, where Escoffier

inscribed the book "*à mon cher ami A. Gastaud, sympathique souvenir.*"

They met again when Escoffier visited New York in 1930 for the opening of the Hotel Pierre—an event important enough to rate a report in the *New York Times*.

HONORS PRINCE OF CHEFS.
The Knickerbocker Chef Names
a Dish for Escoffier.

To commemorate the recent visit of M. Escoffier, prince of chefs, A. Gastaud, chef of the Hotel Knickerbocker, has been toiling on a new dish, which shall bear the name of the noted cook. After three weeks of experimenting and study, Gastaud has evolved Guinea Hen à la Escoffier. He believes the new dish is worthy of the renowned chef after whom it is named.

(If you'd like to try cooking Guinea Hen à la Escoffier, Gastaud's recipe—not a very difficult one— appears at the back of this book.)

Gastaud, like Marcel Proust, can claim to have inspired literature, though it was a fame he might have preferred to avoid. When he took over the $28 million

Waldorf-Astoria hotel in 1931, at the height of the Great Depression, poet Langston Hughes protested at such luxury coexisting with soup kitchens. His poem "Advertisement for the Waldorf-Astoria" borrowed lines from an ad in *Vanity Fair* that explained "the famous Oscar Tschirky is in charge of banqueting. Alexandre Gastaud is chef."

> *Take a room at the new Waldorf, you down-and-outers-sleepers in charity's flop-houses where God pulls a long face, and you have to pray to get a bed.*
> *They serve swell board at the Waldorf-Astoria.*
> *Look at the menu, will you:*
> > *gumbo creole*
> > *crabmeat in cassolette*
> > *boiled brisket of beef*
> > *small onions in cream*
> > *watercress salad*
> > *peach melba*
> *Have luncheon there this afternoon, all you jobless.*

B ack home after talking to Boris, I took down my copy of *Le Guide Culinaire*. It contained directions

for making crèmes, purées, potages, and consommés—
but no *soupe à l'oignon*. I located it eventually, among
the *garbures*—thick soups, full of vegetables, pieces of
meat, and even bread, either mashed into the soup or
toasted and floated on top. "To be served in a restaurant," Escoffier suggested, "the *garbure à l'oignon* is
given a gratin, either on the surface or in the soup itself.
This '*Garbure à la Cooper*' is described elsewhere."

I turned to "Garbure-Cooper"—and there it was,
the *soupe à l'oignon* I knew. Escoffier summarizes it with
his usual brevity.

> *GARBURE-COOPER. A soup of onions*
> *immersed in a white consommé. The onions are*
> *well fried in butter. Pass them through a* chinois
> *and press down well. Pour the soup into deep bowls,*
> *garnish with rounds of bread, cover the surface*
> *abundantly with cheese,* arroser *with melted butter*
> *and grill till browned.*

Who was "Cooper"? I never found out. A *chinois*
(a Chinese) is a flattened conical strainer, named for its
resemblance to an East Asian "patty hat." But *arroser*
means "to drench," as with a hose. Should I really *drench*
the cheese with melted butter? And how did I make "a

white consommé"? Belatedly I followed Boris's advice and turned to page one, chapter one. And there it was: directions for making a white consommé for ten people. About half that should be enough. Mentally halving the ingredients, I took a pen and pad, and began a lengthy shopping list.

U sed to my odd requests, the butcher in the Marché Saint-Germain still looked puzzled.

"Bones? No meat? Just bones?"

"They're for a bouillon."

"How much did you say?"

"Three kilos?"

"Three kilos!"

He shook his right hand vigorously, as if he'd touched something hot. Uniquely French, the gesture signifies shock, respect, or admiration. The price paid for a new car, how badly someone broke a leg, or a well-filled pair of jeans can all inspire this gestural "Ow!" I responded with a shrug. Often with the French, words just get in the way.

The next day, he handed over a lumpy seven-pound sack. I reached for my wallet. He shook his head. "*Cadeau*," he said. A gift.

Following Escoffier's directions, I set the oven to 150 degrees centigrade, put the bones in a baking dish, added a chopped onion and some garlic cloves, and left them to roast for three hours. They emerged beaded with fat forced out of the marrow by the sustained heat. More fat pooled in the bottom of the dish, flavored by the caramelized garlic and onions.

"*How* many kilos of bones?"

I poured both into a bowl and transferred the bones to my biggest pot. In with them went three carrots, a couple of parsnips, three onions, two sticks of celery, three leeks, a bay leaf, parsley stalks, peppercorns, a handful of sea salt, and seven liters of water, enough to fill the pot to the brim. Bringing the mixture to a boil, I reduced the heat to a simmer, skimmed the froth that rose to the surface, and replaced the lid. I'd already spent half a day reading directions and shopping for ingredients. Just another five hours of cooking, and I could start really making the soup.

Eighteen

First Catch Your Market

> . . . *the markets with their pyramids of fruit, the turns of the seasons, the sides of beef hanging from the hooks, the hill of spices, and the towers of bottles and preserves, all of the flavors and colors, all the smells and all the stuff, the tide of voices—water, metal, wood, clay—the bustle, the haggling, and contriving as old as time.*
>
> Octavio Paz, *I Speak of the City*

Soupe à l'oignon became famous as the meal of workers at Paris's meat and produce market, Les Halles. Since opening in 1183, the complex grew until it sprawled across twenty-five acres of the Right Bank. In 1850, Baron Haussmann, as part of redesigning Paris, brought it up-to-date. To replace the jumble of sheds, he had Victor Baltard design ten glass-sided pavilions with metal roofs supported on delicate cast-iron columns—the *halles*, or halls, that gave the market its name. These survived until its demolition in 1971, when, scandalously, most were sold as scrap iron to the Japanese at a knockdown price.

Almost everything eaten in Paris passed through Les Halles, brought in overnight by horse and cart from outlying farms and abattoirs, or by train from farther away; the market had its own siding. A suburban farmer would load his wagon in the dark, climb onto the seat, and nudge his old horse in the direction of the city's distant glow. Émile Zola's novel *The Belly of Paris* opens with a description of what followed:

> *In the silence of a deserted avenue, wagons stuffed with produce made their way towards Paris, their thudding wheels rhythmically echoing off the houses sleeping behind the rows of elm trees meandering on either side of the road. At the pont de Neuilly, a cart full of cabbages and another full of peas met up with eight carts of turnips and carrots coming in from Nanterre. The horses, their heads bent low, led themselves with their lazy, steady pace, a bit slowed by the slight uphill climb. Up on the carts, lying on their stomachs in the vegetables, wrapped in their black-and-grey striped wool coats, the drivers slept with the reins in their fists.*

Early risers in Paris were used to convoys of such carts clopping across the Seine toward the market, their drivers still asleep.

Off-loaded into the pavilions, sorted, priced, and put on display, the produce and meat flowed out again in the barrows and baskets of hoteliers, restaurateurs, shopkeepers, and housewives. Even the authors of the 1931 *Guide des Plaisirs à Paris*, written for French visitors rather than foreign tourists, recommended a visit. In a way that is typically Gallic, it pictured the market as something inspiring, a living exhibition of France's natural wealth, its *patrimoine*.

You'll see the whole range of colors, from the somber green of vegetables to the garish red of bloody meat, the heaps of baskets, big and small, and the handcarts, pushed around by strapping lads not afraid of their weighty loads.

Les Halles at 7 a.m., 1910s

These porters, called *forts*—"strongs"—earned their license by showing they could muscle 440 pounds, the weight of two grown men, on a wooden hand truck. For a few weeks in 1928, George Orwell tried it but didn't have the strength, so he quit to become a hotel *plongeur*, or "diver"—slang for dishwasher. *Forts* in the meat market were expected to carry the carcass of a whole pig or sheep balanced on their heads. An American visitor wrote, "Never shall I forget the sight of three huge meat-handlers, their long white aprons and turbaned heads smeared with blood, standing like three murderers out of a melodrama of the Middle Ages, and amiably discussing politics."

As well as thirteen thousand regular employees, Les Halles supported a dozen smaller communities, including the urban poor. They crowded around the outskirts until the bell, or *cloche*, rang at 8:00 a.m., signaling the end of trading. Then they poured in, scavenging bruised fruit, discarded vegetables, and scraps of meat. Even today, the French still call the homeless *clochards*—bell people.

Other appetites were also catered for. Rent-by-the-hour *hôtels de passe* filled the surrounding streets where, day and night, prostitutes loitered, ready to satisfy any *forts* with energy to spare. As a little girl, my mother-in-law, being rushed past such a group by her nanny, asked why these brightly dressed women were standing in such numbers. Improvising quickly, the nanny said, "They're engaged girls, waiting for their fiancés to finish work."

The "fiancés," called "*mecs*" from *maquereaux*, or mackerel—their tight flashy suits resembled the shiny striped skin of that fish—hung out in nearby basement bars, from where they could keep an eye on their girls and collect their takings. The same places were patronized by *apaches*, named from the Native Americans brought to Paris in Wild West shows. The 1950s musical and film *Irma la Douce*, set in the nonexistent rue Casanova, sweetens and romanticizes a sordid and dangerous milieu.

Among the pimps' dives, the "most poisonous of all," in the words of American writer Julian Street, was the Caveau des Innocents at 15 rue des Innocents—today ironically the headquarters of the Lancia Motor Club. "It consisted of a vaulted cellar with a doorway so low that one had to stoop on entering, and a series of narrow little rooms in which congregated many desperate characters." The piano player was a *bossu*, or hunchback. Waiters and musicians in such places were often physically handicapped. Afflictions that might discon-

Le Caveau des Innocents

cert clients in respectable establishments were welcomed by criminals. Rubbing the back of a *bossu* was believed to bring luck, particularly to gamblers; sufferers from the condition loitered near casinos, charging for the service.

In 1910, dancer Maurice Mouvet was taken to the Innocents by a friend. "It was lighted by green and red lights," he recalled. "They were oil lamps, and their smoke-covered shades leered down from the walls with a baleful glare. There was sand on the filthy floor and rough deal tables about the room. At these tables, groups of apaches were playing poker with their knives open on the table beside them."

During the evening, a *mec* grabbed one of the *poules*, or chicks, and performed a variation on the Rough

Dance, a country romp in which a couple playfully bumped and jostled one another. At the Innocents, the dance became more like a brawl, the girl begging for her man's attention, he shoving her away, even throwing her to the floor, only to have her crawl back and clutch his leg adoringly. Impressed, Mouvet paid the man to teach him the steps and created the Apache Dance, which became a feature of night club shows around the world.

Emile Zola christened Les Halles "*le ventre de Paris*"—"the belly of Paris." That belly needed feeding—the task of such all-night cafés as Au Chien qui Fume (The Smoking Dog), Au Père Tranquille (The Quiet Father), and Au Pied de Cochon (The Pig Foot)—*au* in this case signifying "at the sign of."

Socialites often joined the crowd at the end of a long night, slumming or looking for "a bit of rough." The *Guide des Plaisirs* warned that the locals might not be as naïve as they looked. "The regulars here will sometimes ambush susceptible strangers on the stairs, persuade them to buy them dinner, then disappear at the end of the meal."

"The crowd is extremely mixed," it continued, "and very amusing. A woman in a chic evening dress will

sit next to a working girl *en cheveux*." *En cheveux*—
"bareheaded"—was a slur: no respectable woman appeared in public without a hat, even around Les Halles.
Visiting Montmartre, not regarded as particularly gen-
teel, a British writer noticed that his lady companion "attracted more attention than she liked, for she was hatless
and in evening dress, and all the others of her sex we
saw were largely covered. In Paris, of an evening, two
cherries and a piece of velvet are sufficient headgear, but
[wearing] no headgear, except at the Opera, is looked
upon as odd."

Au Chien qui Fume enforced no dress code. It was
too busy, even in the small hours. "At 3 a.m.," explained
the *Guide des Plaisirs*, "the ground floor, the small
dining rooms on the first floor and the private rooms
are all filled with people eating supper." According to
Julian Street, "The crowds stayed until morning, dancing, singing the latest ribald songs, occasionally breaking chairs and bottles, and sometimes shedding blood."
All this was tolerated as good for business. Burly waiters kept order, and if the occasional pickpocket or whore
slipped by, that just added to the atmosphere.

At these cafés, almost everyone ate what *New Yorker*
magazine correspondent Janet Flanner called "the rich,
brunette onion soup." Nothing fought off a hangover

Onion Soup outside Les Halles, 1889

better, or more effectively revived the libido. It was never off the menu. Even when the cook had gone home, an apprentice could fill a bowl from the pot simmering at the back of the stove, float a slab of oven-dried bread on top, cover it in grated cheese, and brown it under the grill.

Some improved the soup with "a hair of the dog" by following the custom of *chabrot*—pouring red wine into the dregs to swill out the last scraps of bread and onion. Practiced since childhood, *chabrot* turned many young Frenchmen into alcoholics, the painter Maurice Utrillo among them. Others claimed that wine, like soup, was good for the health. According to an old rhyme, *"Après la soupe un coup de vin / C'est un écu de moins au médecin"*—A glass of wine after the soup means one less coin for the doctor.

In 1971, Les Halles relocated in a characterless but healthier complex at Rungis. The redevelopers created a park covering an ugly multilevel shopping mall and railway interchange. The prostitutes moved a few blocks east, to rue St. Denis, and most of the restaurants closed. Of the few that remain, some still serve onion soup, but the spirit of Les Halles didn't survive demolition—except, briefly, in one form. While it was still a building site, flowers and vegetables sprouted from the ripped-up earth. Many varieties hadn't been cultivated in an age. They sprang from seeds scattered over centuries—ghosts of the old market, clinging defiantly to life.

A round 10:00 p.m., it was time to take the bouillon off the heat. It wasn't white—more a pale gold—but Escoffier used "white" to distinguish it from the essences that provided a base for rich *daubes*, or stews, of wild boar or hare, in which the blood of the animal blended with the bouillon.

I dredged out and discarded the bones and vegetables. Their flavor remained in the broth, which I poured through a deep colander lined with a wet tea towel. Though it had looked clear, the straining had left a thick residue. After that, the soup, reduced now to three liters from the original five, went into the fridge, and I went to bed.

The next morning, a layer of hard white fat covered the bowl, like ice on a pond. Under it, the natural gelatin of the bones had turned the stock to a golden jelly. I broke up the fat and added it to what I'd extracted during baking. This "dripping" was an indispensable ingredient for greasing a *côte du boeuf* or creating perfect roast potatoes, crunchy outside but with interiors of the consistency the French call *fondant*—melting. How right country cooks had been to save such by-products. *Sot-l'y-laisse*—the stupid leave them.

I could have served the jellied bouillon as it was, cold, chopped up, garnished with shreds of raw vegetable and a scattering of fresh chopped herbs. But having come this far, I wasn't about to shy at the last fence.

Setting the pot on low heat, I watched the jelly dissolve into a swirling yellow consommé, shimmering with the little fat that remained. I checked the clock: 9:00 a.m. There was now a real possibility we might have *soupe à l'oignon* for lunch.

I ran half a kilo of white onions through the food processor, filling a bowl with the transparent slices. Melting half that amount of sweet butter in one of my Le Creuset cast-iron orange-enameled cocottes, the Porsches of kitchen tools, I added the onion, with a spoonful of sugar to hasten caramelization. After forty minutes on low heat, it was a deep gold. I drained off the excess butter, poured in a glass of cognac, let the alcohol vaporize, then stirred in a large spoonful of flour. Butter and flour combined to create the roux on which any sauce or thick soup is founded.

Once it browned, I trickled in the bouillon, stirring to prevent lumps. The clear broth became an opaque but still golden soup that showed plenty of onions when stirred but wasn't, like some café versions, clogged with them.

While it simmered, I put a dozen pieces of three-day-old bread into a low oven to crisp. Old bread is another of those ingredients that "the stupid leave." To use fresh bread in onion soup is inviting disaster. The underside goes to mush while the upper surface bonds with the cheese to become yellow leather.

It was time for the last touches: a handful of Gruyère stirred into the pot, followed by a raw onion grated fine. Unlike some suggested additions—an egg beaten with port is surely the worst—the cheese and onion would remind the palate of the essential ingredients that cooking had transformed. I ladled the soup into deep bowls, floated a slice of the dried bread on each, moistened (but not "drenched") with butter drained from the onion. Heaping grated Gruyère liberally on top, I placed the bowls under the grill, though not so close that the cheese would burn before it melted.

The aroma of toasting cheese, one of the most seductive in the world, filled the kitchen. As the cheese began to brown, I removed the bowls and placed them on a tray. At this moment in a French household, one called "*À table!*"—to the table. But for once, I reverted to my Anglo-Saxon roots and announced, "Soup's on!"

Was it worth the effort? Well, everyone loved it. Marie-Dominique, Louise, and I devoured two big bowls each, down to the last drop of the three liters I'd made.

Did it taste better than the version at Au Pied de Cochon? Deliciously so. There was a depth to the flavor that made each spoonful an experience. If you could chew a liquid, that is what we did.

But for all its flavor, there was something absurd about having spent two days making it. For two days, I'd lived like a *sous chef* of a century before, baking, boiling, filtering, skimming, falling into bed to rise the next morning and start again. Because I'd chosen to do so, it was fun. But if I had no choice? There were more fulfilling ways to spend one's time.

No cook is so foolish that he won't use a packaged product if he can't tell the result from fresh. Robert Carrier, the British celebrity food writer of the 1970s and author of *Great Dishes of the World*, insisted that canned pineapple juice was indistinguishable in texture and flavor from the fresh-crushed fruit. Unless you can cook green peas within a few hours of picking, the frozen product is far superior, since freezing preserves the sugars that otherwise turn to starch. Alice B. Toklas, the most traditional of cooks, was a late but enthusiastic convert to American cake mixes, albeit with "improvements." She gave Betty Crocker pound cake a frosting made with the whiskey liqueur Drambuie.

In Escoffier's memoirs, I'd discovered an obscure detail of his military service. As the Prussians besieged Metz, he scoured the town for supplies. After corralling a flock of chickens, geese, ducks, and turkeys, he managed to grab a sheep and a goat, twenty kilos of salt, and four large jars of plum jam, which served as a sweetener when sugar disappeared.

Since 1795 the French army had been trying to perfect some way of preserving food for military use, but until then had succeeded only with glass jars. Escoffier found that the Prussians ate canned products developed by the chemist and pioneering nutritionist Baron Justus von Liebig. He seized all he could find, including sardines and tuna fish in oil—"a fortunate inspiration," he wrote, "that caused no complaints from my officers, as they ended up being the best served of all the chiefs of staff." When the war ended, he encouraged the development of canning and routinely used canned and bottled food in his hotels and restaurants.

Von Liebig also invented a meat extract and a powdered bouillon that could be reconstituted with hot water. Undoubtedly, Escoffier knew these products. It's even conceivable he employed them in the field and during the siege. Could it be that the greatest chef of his day, the man who literally wrote the book on haute cuisine, used . . . stock cubes?

Nineteen

First Catch Your Anchovy

*How delicious, to a schoolboy's healthy appetite, sixty
years ago, was the potted meat at breakfast in my grandmother's old Wiltshire home. Neat little white pots, with
a crust of yellow butter suggesting the spicy treat beneath,
beef, ham, or tongue, handiwork of the second or third
kitchen maid . . .*
    "A. Potter," in *Pottery: Home Made Potted Foods,*
    Meat and Fish Pastes, Savoury Butters and others.
    The Wine and Food Society, London, 1946

It's easy, in planning a great meal, to forget the importance of detail. After the table had been set for a
banquet in an aristocratic home, the butler would tour
it with a measuring stick, checking that the knives,
forks and spoons, glasses, and plates were all precisely equidistant from one another; that the napkins
were correctly and consistently folded; that no smudge
marred a wineglass.

On the few occasions when I saw this process in action, I was reminded of the care with which the priest aligned the objects on the altar before Mass. More than the devil was in the details; there was a touch of sanctity as well. Respecting precision and ritual is a sort of reverence.

In the 1970s, when I lived in a village in the English county of Suffolk, I timed my trips to London to catch the 4:00 p.m. train home—the only service that offered afternoon tea.

British Rail provided a special dining carriage for the purpose—one of the last, to judge from the bald spots on its plush seats, the chips along the edges of the varnished tabletops, and the brass fittings blurred from decades of rubbing. Even the waiter's high-cut white linen jacket, known as a "bum-freezer," was threadbare at the edges from too much starching and ironing. When the old carriage was shunted off to oblivion, the tradition of afternoon tea would expire with it, replaced by a bleak standup snack bar. This made it even more important to enjoy the experience while we could.

In more gracious times, tea was less a meal than a ritual, almost a sacrament. One "took" tea, as a Catholic "takes" communion or a nun "takes the veil."

On the 4:00 p.m., conventions were strictly observed. A few minutes before departure, the lone waiter came through and asked each passenger, "Are you taking tea?" Those who answered no were politely ordered out. We who remained received a thick china cup, saucer, and plate, and a spoon—all decades old and dulled by long service. A jug of milk and a bowl of sugar were placed on each table. Just as the train glided out of the station, the waiter passed down the car with a giant metal teapot, filling our cups.

Then came the treats.

First, a basket of buttered bread, wholemeal and white, sliced diagonally, crusts still attached. We took one of each; two of the same color implied ungentlemanly excess. When slices of fruitcake followed, those who'd chosen bread and butter usually declined, saving their appetite for the next course: tea cakes. These sweet rolls were sliced in two, toasted, and buttered. The sugar-crusted tops were tastier than the bottoms, but everyone dutifully took one of each.

Finally, the waiter returned with a basket of sandwiches.

How to describe British sandwiches?

Somewhere in Whitehall there is probably a manual, dating back to Queen Victoria, that defines the rules for preparing a sandwich—known, despite the bread being invariably square, as a "round."

A round of sandwiches consists of two slices of soft white bread, crusts trimmed off. A scraping of butter prevents the bread from becoming soggy from the filling, which is usually cucumber, peeled but not seeded, sliced paper-thin, patted dry on a linen tea towel, then dusted with white pepper. Cucumber sandwiches are the test of a tea. Cooks in the best houses cut them in "fingers," each a perfect mouthful. In 1948, Queen Mary invited film director Terence Young to Buckingham Palace to discuss his cryptic first film, *Corridor of Mirrors*. Young didn't remember much of the conversation but never forgot the refreshments. "Those cucumber sandwiches! My dear chap! Thin as razor blades."

The sandwiches on the 4:00 p.m. from Liverpool Street, though not up to Buckingham Palace standard, were respectably thin. Fillings never varied: cucumber of course, cress, egg salad, and anchovy paste. They arrived cut diagonally into quarters. It was understood that each of us should take four quarters, one of each filling. So imagine my astonishment when, one afternoon, as the basket was passed, the passenger opposite, a complete stranger, said, "Ah! Fish paste! My favorite"—and helped himself to *four quarters of fish paste*!

Time froze. My neighbor, also a stranger, turned

toward me just as I turned toward him. Our eyes met.
Our eyebrows raised in unison. Well!

That's when I realized I was turning into an Englishman.

S ecretly, I sympathized with our greedy companion.
Because I, too, liked anchovy paste.

Americans grew up on sandwiches spread with
peanut butter and jam. This mixture was unknown in
Europe or its colonies. Very occasionally, we got sugar
sandwiches—white bread and butter scattered with
sugar or, on special occasions, with multicolor *nonpareils*: what Americans call "sprinkles" but which we
knew as "hundreds-and-thousands."

Mostly, however, our sandwiches were filled with
savory pastes of ham, fish, shrimp, processed cheese, or
occasionally a black goo, extracted from yeast, called
Marmite in Britain and Vegemite in Australia. Although
Vegemite resembled axle grease and was so salty it made
you salivate like a bloodhound, it sizzled with vitamin B
and so was a fixture of many Australian tables, next to
the pepper and salt.

These days, anchovy paste comes in tubes, but I remember it in small glass jars molded vaguely in the form of a barrel, with a brassy metal lid. I liked the paste spread on buttered toast, particularly the fingers—known in Britain as "soldiers"—that I dipped into boiled eggs.

Anchovy paste in Australia, where the anchovy itself was unknown, followed the fashion to imitate things British—which, by definition, were superior to anything we might have produced. In this case, the model was "potted meats": cooked meat or fish pounded to a paste with pepper, salt, and herbs, then pressed into small china pots and covered with melted butter to keep the contents fresh.

When I moved to Britain, I looked for anchovy paste but quickly found a better alternative. In 1828 a resourceful grocer named John Osborn developed a paste specifically for military officers overseas. Hard, salty, and spicy, it came in a white porcelain pot that evoked homemade potted meats. On the lid, black letters spelled out the trade name: Patum Peperium. Though this sounds like it should be Latin for "peppery paste," the words mean nothing in any known language. In any event, the product was better known under its nom de guerre "The Gentleman's Relish."

I bought my first pot at London's best grocers, Fortnum and Mason. In those days, its salesmen still wore tail coats and striped trousers, like ushers at a fashionable wedding. All the same, one of them accepted my money without asking for proof that I was a gentleman, and I left with the slightly furtive sense of having Got Away with something.

After that, Patum Peperium was always on the table. I spread it on toast, stirred it into stews, and used it in cocktail snacks. For a pre-dinner canapés at my banquet, I couldn't imagine anything tastier than squares of toast spread with Gentleman's Relish and topped with a quail's egg, hard-boiled and sliced in half. *The New Yorker*, famous for its fact checking, recently called Gentleman's Relish "a lip-puckering anchovy paste made from a secret recipe in a factory in Elsenham, England." Not so, I'm afraid. In this era of free information, the formula is available online (and in the recipe section at the rear of this book).

M y weakness for anchovy paste helps explain why my friend Christopher and I were standing on the railway station at Perpignan, in the deep southwest of France, reading the words *Centre de l'Universe* painted in large white letters on the platform.

On the wall overhead, a photograph showed surrealist painter Salvador Dalí striding down this very platform with Gala, his wife, on their way from Spain to Paris with a cargo of fresh insanity. Though he never commanded so much as a canoe, Dalí wore the all-white uniform of an admiral of the Spanish navy, a privilege conferred on him by General Franco, Spain's fascist head of state, whom he extravagantly admired.

Dalí claimed that, while changing trains at Perpignan on September 19, 1963, he experienced "a sort of cosmic ecstasy," with powerful sexual overtones. Scholars speculate that this must have been a prodigious erection, followed perhaps by a spontaneous orgasm. In his autobiography, Dalí wasn't that specific.

> *It is always at Perpignan station, when Gala is making arrangements for the paintings to follow us by train, that I have my most unique ideas. It is the arrival at Perpignan station that marks an absolute mental ejaculation which then reaches its greatest and most sublime speculative height. On this 19th of September, I had a kind of ecstasy that was cosmogonic and even stronger than preceding ones. I had an exact vision of the constitution of the universe.*

He incorporated his vision into a 1965 canvas called *Mystique de la gare de Perpignan*, which shows him blown literally sky-high by the force of his revelation. The French railway system, not to be outdone, commemorated the event by painting *"Centre de l'Universe"* on its platform. I can't quite see this happening at Grand Central or Charing Cross.

This far southwest in France, so close to the Spanish border, erotic arousal comes with the territory, particularly if it involves the railways. In August 1999, art historian Catherine Millet toured the area with her husband, the novelist Jacques Henric. Mainly she wanted to visit the grave of Walter Benjamin, who wrote the influential essay "The Work of Art in the Age of Mechanical Reproduction" and committed suicide here in 1940 while fleeing the Nazis.

In addition to being a respected writer on art and editor of an influential monthly, Millet was, as she had just revealed in her bestseller *La Vie Sexuelle de Catherine M.*, a tireless sexual athlete and a regular on the Parisian group-sex circuit. She also enjoyed exposing herself nude in the open air and being photographed doing so. At Walter Benjamin's grave, she posed naked while Henric photographed her. They then went to the Port-Bou railway station, where, as the Barcelona express roared through, she stood with her dress wide open to show the speeding and no doubt incredulous passengers that she was wearing nothing else. Once again, Henric captured the moment.

Millet's sexual games are harmless, and indeed, like the lady herself, rather charming, as well as being witty comments on the way in which photography changed the nature of art, which is what Benjamin dealt with in his essay. Nudity, real or reproduced, as a means of communication among intellectuals isn't uncommon in modern French culture. Ned Rorem introduced himself to fellow composer (and fellow gay man) Benjamin Britten by mailing him a seminude self-portrait. Once this got around, people who wished to meet Rorem, including women, sent him similar photographs of themselves, until he was forced to remove his address from the phone book. On another occasion, the countess Marie-Laure de Noailles, patroness of Man Ray, Luis Buñuel, and Rorem, wished to show her disapproval of the fiancée chosen by one of her protegées. Quietly leaving the salon of her mansion on Place des États-Unis, she reappeared a few moments later in the doorway naked, posed there for a moment, then disappeared again, to return fully clothed. "I just wanted you to know," she told the bemused couple, "what a real Frenchwoman looked like."

•   •   •

Had any intellectual passing through Perpignan that morning offered a repeat of the countess's gesture or Millet's exposure, Christopher and I would probably have missed it. We were too busy sprinting across four platforms to board the slow train for a thirty-minute trip to the port of Collioure, center of France's anchovy industry.

Christopher once lived near there and had happy memories of its hospitality, its wine, its cuisine, and, of course, its anchovies. But as I clambered onto the train, the absurdity of the expedition struck me. To travel seven hours across France to discover the source of anchovy paste? Wasn't this as strange as dressing as an admiral or exposing oneself to a train full of tourists? It

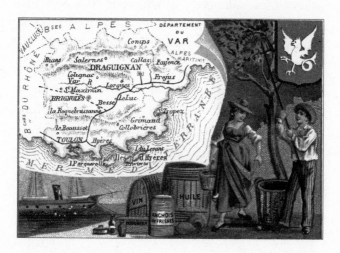

seems that the region of Catalonia, which encompasses cities such as Barcelona on the Spanish side of the border and Collioure and Perpignan on the French side, induces excesses of this sort.

Collioure came well recommended. Mark Kurlansky in his history *Salt* described it as a busy community where the locals, from May to October, set out daily in vividly painted boats, called *catalans*, to fish for anchovies, which they filleted by hand and salted down in wooden casks. The rest of the year was spent raising grapes for wine and awaiting the moment when the anchovies arrived serenely at maturity.

This Friday in December, however, Collioure had an air of lassitude, even despair. With no cabs at the railway station, we trundled our bags downhill toward the town center. On the way, we passed the bullring. Just some bleachers enclosed in a flimsy metal screen, it hardly deserved the name. In any event, it was now closed indefinitely, since the Catalonian government had just banned the corrida—not out of compassion for the animals but as a gesture to the increasingly vociferous animal-rights lobby. Beyond, the main route into town was ripped up for resurfacing and the laying of new sewer pipes. We had to pick our way among bulldozers and trench diggers. Nevertheless, though it was only midday, not a single worker was in sight nor would there be any until Monday.

In ten minutes, we arrived at the Mediterranean.

"It's quieter than I remember," Chris said, looking round the empty quayside.

On one side of the pretty bay, a tower straight out of a pirate fantasy commanded an ocean that, except for a few wavelets rippling on the pebble beach, was motionless. On the opposite point hulked a crumbling stone fortress, the Château Royal, looking as ominous as the Spanish Inquisition. No colorful *catalans* were pulled up on the shingle. As for the local wine industry, interest seemed to end in a couple of cafés, where locals huddled over a *pichet* and studied the lottery results.

A chat with the desk clerk at our hotel brought us up-to-date. In the last three years, Collioure had declined. At one time, Perpignan looked to become the major center of the region, but interest now flowed inexorably across the border to Barcelona, the undisputed magnet for tourism and commerce.

At the same time, the European Union cut the number of days Collioure's anchovy fleet could fish. But the real problem was the anchovies themselves. Some years, they swarmed just offshore. Lately, however, they'd shunned French waters for those of North Africa, so that any fish eaten next year would be mostly Algerian.

Of the once-thriving fleet, only a few boats remained, and a single cannery, run by the Desclaux family since 1903. We wandered uphill to its headquarters through the empty town, past blocks of holiday apartments with every shutter wound down tight. Cafés, restaurants, even pharmacies were closed for the winter, their furniture locked inside behind windows grilled with steel.

Madame Desclaux greeted us warmly in the chilly but meticulously clean white-tiled shop, and led us around the large room next door, kept up as a museum of the trade. In the summer, women gave demonstrations here of how they tore the fish apart with the only instruments sufficiently delicate to tease out those tiny bones: their fingers. But with no anchovies to dissect, we could only ponder the waist-high wooden barrels where filleted fish matured.

We watched a video of Collioure's once-great days and mused on the rows of vividly pictorial but now rusting cans, souvenirs of packers who'd gone out of business. François, madame's husband, appeared in faded denim overalls to guide us through his gallery of anchovy art. The paintings, showing the shingle beach crowded with *catalans*, were mostly amateur, but he did own one work by the most notorious Catalan of them all, a tiny and puzzling drawing of an ant, flamboyantly signed "Dalí." An ant? Not so strange, Christopher explained. To Dalí, ants signified death and decay. As a child, he'd come across a dead bat crawling with ants and been traumatized. Maybe the ant was his wry comment on the decline of Collioure.

Browsing through this mausoleum of the anchovy industry, I could only think: If only *garum* were still in vogue.

Hardly anyone in Collioure would know of *garum*, but in the ancient world, this corner of the Mediterranean was a center for its manufacture. This all-purpose essence was a vital ingredient in Greek and Roman cuisine. Rich in proteins, minerals, amino acids, vitamin B, and a natural form of the flavor enhancer monosodium glutamate, *garum* was the universal elixir. It gave savor to meat and fish dishes, and even desserts. It could be mixed with wine or water, both for refreshment and as a medicine. Users swore it cured dysentery, diarrhea, constipation, and ulcers. It also removed freckles, body hair, and even healed dog bites.

Improbably, *garum* was made by mixing fish guts or whole small fish with salt, packing the mixture into vats and leaving them in the open for weeks. The stink of a *garum* factory must have been toxic, yet the liquid that rose to the top of the vats after a few months was clear, golden, fragrant, and salty/sweet. Worcestershire sauce, Gentleman's Relish, Vegemite, and the Vietnamese fish sauce Nuoc Mam, essential to many Asian dishes, all descend from *garum*.

The Spanish variety, fermented in the blazing Catalan sun, was particularly prized. At one time, it was shipped in thousands of spindle-shaped clay amphorae from ports such as Collioure to every corner of the Roman Empire. And who could say it wouldn't find a new market today? Part snake oil, part ketchup, part kitchen cleanser; organic, vegetarian, gluten- and GM-free, it was the perfect twenty-first-century product. *A Thousand Household Uses. All Natural Ingredients. No Home Should Be Without It.* But no doubt a hundred European Union regulations existed to make its manufacture illegal, if not criminal.

Loaded with samples of Desclaux products, and in desperate need of a drink, Chris and I stopped at our hotel to drop off our souvenirs.

"Have you visited the Christmas fair yet?" the desk clerk asked. "You must go to the fair. It's in the château."

With nothing much else to do till supper, we climbed into the crumbling pile of the Château Royal. Repeatedly rebuilt and refortified, this horrid pile had known nothing but grief since Wamba the Visigoth laid siege to it in 673. Most recently, it had imprisoned refugees from the Spanish Civil War during the 1930s and opponents of the pro-Nazi Vichy regime during World War II. Today, it's a training center for commandos. One could see why. In its niches, oubliettes, and staircases, winding, narrow, and unlit, you'd never notice the man in the ski mask until he slit your throat.

Determined not to be dispirited by the air of medieval menace, the locals had drenched the château in Christmas cheer. Former torture chambers and dungeons became brightly lit boutiques where vendors urged us to sample foie gras, gingerbread, honey, jam, and cheese—though nothing, oddly, related to anchovies. Larger chambers had become bars, with barrels instead of tables, and shelves piled with bottles. At last we could taste the elusive local wine—most of it, however, made over the border in Spain. Fortunately, the merchants followed a generous Spanish tradition. None of the bottles clustered on the barrel-heads had corks, and the pouring girls could barely wait to refill our glasses.

We reeled out into the ancient courtyard, overlooked by battlements. Adding to the medieval atmosphere, a gaggle of geese milled around, honking hoarsely. Two saddled donkeys drowsed near the wall, ready to give rides to children. Just as a doubtful little boy was being placed on its back, one of these animals defecated explosively. The child wailed in panic as glossy lumps tumbled from under the animal's tail, an introduction to the equine digestive system that probably scarred him for life.

Geographically we might still be in France, but everything around us smelled of Spain. Though the plains and windmills of La Mancha were hundreds of kilometers south, Don Quixote could well have come clacking into the courtyard on his bony Rocinante with Sancho trailing behind. To the deluded Don, the château would be a palace and its shoppers a crowd of beautiful women and handsome men in opulent court dress. Perhaps that's how it also looked to the people climbing the narrow stone staircases, peering into brightly lit shops. They were having a wonderful time.

Country towns don't differ much. In Australia we'd looked forward just as much to the annual agricultural show, with its stalls of produce, its displays of prize-winning homemade jams and lopsided cakes, but above all its traveling carnival. I paid sixpence to gape at the fetus of a two-headed calf floating in its jar of yellow fluid, and stared, flushed, at the wobbling white belly of a middle-aged lady as she performed a sketchy approximation of the *danse du ventre* to lure our fathers and uncles into the sexier show that was "all happening on the inside."

"What they need is a midway," I said to Chris. "A Ghost Train and a hoochy-coochy show. They'd liven up the place."

He pointed toward the gate. "Maybe this is it."

A dozen aged ladies and gentlemen in traditional Catalan dress of drab black—the women with lace caps, the men with red hats—were clustered around a harmonium. As it wheezed into life, they began to harmonize, more or less, in almost toneless unison. We were being treated to a performance of what passed in this region for Christmas carols.

"Catalan music tends to be monotonous," Chris said apologetically.

Just then, they hit a particularly sour note. The geese honked in approval. The singers glared but droned on. Chris and I both started to laugh. Surrealism was building up around us, like a drift of invisible snow. I looked up at the battlements, where it would not have surprised me to see Catherine Millet wearing nothing but Wellington boots and gardening gloves. Instead, I saw a man in white peering down. Could that be an admiral's uniform? Had the great Catalan returned—to commune with the shades of lost anchovies perhaps, and to visit his ant, or in the hope of another transcendental experience on the train? *Ola*, Don Salvador!

Twenty

First Catch Your *Noisette*

I like my coffee!
Like my coffee sweet and hot.
Won't let nobody meddle
With my coffee pot.

Old blues

Coffee coffee coffee. How do I love thee? Let me count the ways. Nescafé at dawn, drunk from a mug with a silly design; half milk, and the sugar barely dissolved, but most of it gulped in a swallow, fuel for a morning's work. Or a *crème* in the café on the corner of boulevard Saint-Germain, seething milk poured into an inky *express*, black and white turning beige; water into wine.

Later in the day, *café allongé*—stretched coffee, with extra hot water instead of milk, for a cuppa Java just like they make Back Home. Or my preference, *noisette*—a modest *express* compromised by a dash of milk, the soiled dove of coffees that Italians call *macchiato*, or "stained." Not forgetting the classic *express*, sipped standing at the zinc on a rainy afternoon, the Tour Eiffel a high ghost in the overcast, my neighbor companionably pushing the sugar along the bar, then returning to his dog-eared copy of Boris Vian.

The international language of coffee. Coffee in Indian and Chinese restaurants, so vile it must be revenge for the Raj or the Opium Wars. Dutch coffee, *Douwe Egberts*, so mellow and milky you want to glug it, cup after cup. Turkish coffee—powder, sugar, water; black, gluey, gritty, a liquid confection. Ah, but then the espresso of Italy, Cadillac of coffees. *No, not Cadillac. Porsche*. Brown-black ichor under *crema* thick enough to support the pyramid of sugar from the paper tube for twothreefour*five!* seconds before it's swallowed down. Coffee not so much drunk as inhaled. And the caffeine kick, shivering down your nerves, making your ears sing.

And what about American coffee? The frowns when, on my first stateside visit, I asked for "white coffee." The kindly explanation: "Ah, you mean 'coffee regular.'" Equal confusion from a French waiter at the concept of "iced coffee." Ice and coffee? An unimaginable perversion at that time, but now an omnipresent banality, thanks to Starbucks and its Iced Frappuccino, a cappuccino drugged with vanilla, hazelnut, caramel—coffee in drag, too timid to come out of the closet as what it really is: a milkshake.

And Irish coffee now. Saints preserve us! A different thing entirely. Coffee, sugar, and whiskey, with a dog collar of barely pourable cream. The eighth sacrament, potent enough to raise the dead. So transcendental you'd swear it was invented in the Vatican. In fact, someone at Shannon Airport thought it up to revive passengers stumbling off the first unpressurized, unheated transatlantic flights. The four food groups in a glass—sugar, caffeine, alcohol, fat—served warm to speed their progress into chilled bodies yearning for resurrection.

Coffee coffee coffee. No such thing as a bad cup; just some cups less good.

Always, of course, excepting decaf. Decaf—the essence of disappointment. The fumbled pass that loses the game; the ball that rims the hole but doesn't *quite* drop; the orgasm you just *know* was faked; the mystery you realize on page ten that you've already read. Like crawling into an unmade bed; not finding the matching sock; ordering "no pineapple" on your pizza but getting it just the same. Decaf's the coffee That Couldn't, the coffee of What Might Have Been, of Not Really Our Sort of Thing. Decaf? I say it's spinach, and I say the hell with it.

Paris street vendor of coffee and hot milk, 1880s

This time Boris met me in La Rhumerie. Something between café, restaurant, and bar, its West Indian bungalow look suggests it should be by a beach in Barbados. Instead, it sits at the busy intersection where rue du Four splits off from boulevard Saint-Germain. On a warm Saturday afternoon, this is one of the Left Bank's most fashionable spots, a vantage for people-watching second to none. This wet Wednesday morning in February, however, we were almost alone.

"What are you reading?"

He held up the white-covered oblong paperback: *789 Néologisms de Jacques Lacan.*

"How is it?"

"Gripping. I can't wait to see how it turns out."

"I'm working on coffee," I told him.

"Why?"

"Well, by tradition . . ."

"You don't really think some person went round at the end of a big dinner with a *cafetière?*" He put a finger into the book to mark his place. "You've been to French dinners. If it's in a restaurant, the waiters have gone home; all but the two stuck with clearing your table and giving you *l'addition*. If the meal is in someone's apartment, nobody's anxious to drink black coffee at midnight, always assuming the host can be bothered to make it. Out of eight guests, at least one will be half-asleep in an armchair. Another will have gone home early, pleading a migraine but actually to watch *Mad Men*. Three more will be drunk, two of them arguing politics, and at least one couple will be on the balcony, either snarling at each other—that's if they're married—or exchanging phone numbers if they aren't. Or even if they are. "

I went home and looked it up. As always, he was right. Coffee was not necessarily part of the classic *repas*. In chateaus and stately homes, guests left the dining room after dessert and "went through" to the drawing room. Sometimes the hostess led only the female guests while the men stayed behind to smoke cigars, drink port (always passing the decanter to the left, even if it had to go all the way round the table to reach you), and either assassinate the reputations of absent friends or tell dirty jokes. Either way, coffee didn't play a role.

Nor was coffee part of a big restaurant dinner. Some sample menus in Escoffier's *Le Guide Culinaire* end with *café Turc* (Turkish coffee) or *café double* (like an *express*, in a small cup, the so-called demitasse). More often, however, he served liqueurs, port or brandy, with *mignardises*, *friandises*, or petit fours: tiny cakes, biscuits, candied fruits, or chocolates—the idea lately revived by some restaurants as *café gourmand* (an *express* with a plate of sugary nibbles).

The first people to add milk to coffee were seventeenth-century monks in Vienna who found the Turkish brew too strong and mixed it with cream and honey. It took time for the custom to spread. Coffee was too precious to dilute, although it wasn't uncommon to "improve" or "correct" it with a dash of cognac. "Coffee without brandy," decreed Samuel Beckett, "is like sex without love."

Café au lait became popular in western Europe when women, barred from the coffeehouses of London and the cafés of the Continent, brewed it at home and, as the Viennese monks had done, softened its taste. Because women liked it this way, coffee with milk came to be regarded as effeminate. By the middle of the nineteenth century, French cafés, if asked, would serve it, though purists complained it attracted women into what had been a male culture.

During the siege of Paris in 1871, the abbot of Saint-André noticed that the shortage of both milk and coffee was affecting what he called "the *café au lait* people," who loitered, gossiping and flirting, in the cafés along the new boulevards created by Baron Haussmann. "They believed there was no more coffee to be had," he said with satisfaction, "so they made do with something else, which doesn't appear to have done them any harm." When coffee was scarce, people drank hot milk in the morning. Once coffee returned, a mixture of hot milk and coffee, *café crème*, became the standard breakfast drink. The French still see it that way: one never drinks *café crème* after midday any more than we eat cornflakes.

The Italian espresso invasion briefly overran France in the 1950s. Cafés bought espresso machines but used them to make the same coffee they'd always brewed. The steam tap heated the milk but not so energetically as to produce a serious froth. An Italian hoping for an authentic cappuccino in France is doomed to a long search.

In one of those oddities that make sense only in France, some cafés, beginning during the Nazi occupation, offered a choice of coffee in a cup or a thick, squat glass. This fad, probably due to a shortage of imported china, might have caught on had the tastemakers taken it up. In her 1943 novel *L'Invitée*, Simone de Beauvoir describes the moment when this change in taste and practice could have taken place. A woman and two men in a café—based, at a guess, on de Beauvoir, Jean-Paul Sartre, and Albert Camus—debate whether coffee cools more quickly in cup or glass. One man argues that the surface of evaporation is greater in a glass; the other insists porcelain is a better insulator. "It was amusing when they debated physics like this," reflects the woman. "Usually they had no idea what they were talking about." Eventually, with a combination of contempt and affection, she settles the argument. "They cool at exactly the same rate," she decrees—and, with this literary shrug, severs a thread in the fabric of culture. Coffee in a glass would never be *in*.

When did I first taste coffee? I was about eight, and a precocious reader. The building that contained my father's bakery and our apartment also housed a lending library. By jiggling a connecting door, I was able to slip in after hours and browse the dark book-lined rooms, dipping into volumes that my parents, had they known the contents, would have snatched from my hands.

Along with other puzzling activities, people in these books drank coffee. Our family never did—only tea. Coffee was thought of as too powerful. People who drank tea so strong that a spoon stood up straight in it would grimace at black coffee. All the same, I demanded that my curiosity be satisfied.

Instant coffee had been around since 1938 but not in Australia. Instead, my mother borrowed a flat-sided black bottle from a shelf in my father's bakehouse. I'd seen him use it to flavor the coffee frosting on *éclairs*. On its label, a Scots military officer in full kilt took his ease before a tent while a turbaned Sikh respectfully served him afternoon coffee—made, it was implied, from the contents of this bottle, called Camp Coffee.

Camp hardly deserved the definition, since only 4 percent was coffee. The rest was water, sugar, and an extract from the chicory plant, whose bulbous roots, dried and pulverized, resemble coffee, though minus the caffeine. In hard times, chicory was often added to stretch the precious beans.

During the wartime shortage of coffee, essences such as Camp had flourished. Those who had known the real thing became nostalgic, even slightly manic, for the lost hit of real caffeine. In 1947, Ian Fleming, not yet creator of James Bond, wrote an article for the literary magazine *Horizon* about the joys of relocating from postwar Britain to Jamaica, where he'd just bought a house. He particularly praised the island's Blue Mountain coffee.

> *You will drink this coffee cold-distilled. That is, the coffee, freshly ground, is percolated over and over again with cold water until a thin black treacle is produced. This is very strong and contains all the aroma which, by roasting, would otherwise be lost on the kitchen air. A third of a cup with hot milk or water added will spoil you for all of the more or less tortured brews you drink in England.*

Over the next few months, numerous readers wrote to complain that they'd tried Fleming's method and ended up with nothing but a tired arm and cups of cold water.

The same article described a remote region of the interior called Cockpit Country, inhabited by the Maroons, descendants of Africans enslaved by the Spanish. According to Fleming, these people refused to pay taxes, "the only corner of the British Empire to do so," and established their own government under a leader known simply as the Colonel, whose badge of office was a British army Sam Browne belt. Readers who protested about the coffee suggested that these stories, too, were a product of the "unbounded drink of all sorts" that Fleming cited as another attraction of Jamaica. Both claims disappeared when the piece was reprinted some years later, although the tale of the Colonel and his private empire was either too hard to kill or too good to waste. It inspired the Eurasian arch-criminal with the articulated steel hand in one of Fleming's most successful James Bond adventures, *Doctor No*.

Ironically, Camp Coffee, or at least its label, has a drama of its own. The figure of the Scot was inspired by Major General Sir Hector Macdonald of the Gordon Highlanders. The uneducated son of a Scots farmer, Macdonald became famous for fighting Afghans, savage dervishes in the Sudan, and, finally, in the Boer War, Dutch-German South Africans. His burly frame and bristling mustaches implied rampant heterosexuality, but in 1903 *The New York Herald* revealed he was gay. After hushed-up affairs in Belgium and with a Boer prisoner, "Fighting Mac" was about to be charged with "habitual crimes of misbehavior with several schoolboys" in a British railway carriage. Rather than be disgraced, he shot himself in a Paris hotel.

Camp retained his picture on the label. It's there still. The only change has been racial. The Sikh batman, who once stood respectfully by, now sits next to Macdonald, enjoying his own coffee break. If the brand survives long enough, perhaps we'll see a version in which a dusky hand has crept under Macdonald's kilt.

A little after 11:00 one Saturday night, the phone rang.

"Boris," a voice said curtly.

"Boris?"

It couldn't be Boris. I'd never seen him use a telephone and, if he was asked, would have sworn that he never communicated in any medium more modern than the quill pen.

"You're still looking for that roasted ox?"

Had he rung just to mock my increasingly fruitless quest? It didn't sound like his style.

"You know I am."

"Well, I've found one."

"You're joking." But I knew he wasn't.

"Take down this name. Bugnicourt."

He spelled it out as I wrote it out.

"What is it?"

"A village. Near Douai."

That was in Nord-Pas-de-Calais, the farthest north-eastern point of France before you entered Belgium. In Cabris, I'd been a few miles from Italy, the farthest point southeast before it became Italy. In search of my ultimate meal, I had covered the country from one end to the other. "And what's up there?"

"They're going to roast an ox."

At last! I'd begun to believe that I'd never find one.

"You're sure? It's not just a side of beef? It's really the whole ox?"

"Well, a whole beef anyway. I don't know if it's been castrated. Maybe it's a cow. Does it matter?"

"No, no. Just that it's the whole animal. This is great! When is it?"

"Ah. That's the difficulty."

"Why?"

"Because, it's now."

Twenty-one

First Catch Your Ox

The game's afoot!

Sherlock Holmes, in stories by
Arthur Conan Doyle

In the half hour it took to get ready, Marie-Dominique and I tried to research Bugnicourt—pronounced "Boon-e-core." Its modest and almost perversely uninformative website revealed that the population, at last count (the 2007 census) numbered 954. It was 65 meters above sea level and two hours' drive east-north-east from Paris, most of that along the A1 autoroute that terminates at Calais, the port for vehicle ferry traffic to England and also the point where the Channel Tunnel resurfaces.

There was nothing about roasting oxen.

"Isn't that a bit odd?" Marie-Dominique said. "An event like that, you'd think they would at least mention it."

I could see her point of view. Had Boris been a jokester, he could well have sent us on a wild goose chase. And the more I assured her of his peerless seriousness, the less convincing I sounded.

Just on the off-chance, we rang the Bugnicourt town hall. There was no answer. There wasn't even an answering machine.

"You know small towns," I said. "Everything is word of mouth."

"Why don't we wait until the morning . . . ?"

"It'll all be over in the morning!"

W e got away almost exactly at midnight. But even then, Marie-Dominique wasn't convinced.

"Explain again why they're doing this," she said as we drove along empty streets toward the *périphérique*.

"Roasting an ox? Well, Boris says it's part of a Fête de Boeuf. Apparently it's an annual event. A celebration of . . . well, meat."

"The French need to celebrate meat? Don't they do that with every meal?"

"Not enough, apparently. Somebody seems to think they need encouraging."

"Hmmm."

I could see how urgent, even panicky, my voice sounded. And I knew I hadn't convinced her. But she kept driving. I suppose that's what love means.

Nighttime on a freeway is just as ghostly in France as anywhere else, with the added sense that, even far from cities, the national passions—for order, for the history and riches of France—remain in force. Lightly but insistently, their hand rested on our shoulder.

Periodically our GPS unit emitted a beep, warning us we were being scanned by radar. More frequently, roadside panels warned us to keep our tires inflated, to drive carefully on wet or icy roads, and to rest if we felt tired. To encourage this, the highways of France, though privately owned, are lined with scenic turnoffs called *aires*, picnic spots and rest stops by day, havens at night for truckers to pull in and sleep. We glimpsed them as we passed, tractor trailers from Poland and Hungary, dark blobs within the groves of trees, like sleeping elephants.

Unlike Britain's nationalized highways, where you can drive a hundred miles without a gas pump, toilet, or café, autoroutes, in return for your tolls, offer fuel, sandwiches, fruit, yogurt, water, coffee, tea, chocolate, clean toilets, even, sometimes, a shower. A few stops have children's playgrounds and exercise areas. There's none of the rowdiness of American truck stops of legend: no bar, no jukebox, no pool tables, no whores. In France, and particularly this close to the Channel, truckers behave like the small businessmen they are, and sleep at night, alone. Either they've just got off the ferry and need a nap before pressing on, or they're saving their energy for the dawn drive to Calais and the day's first boat to Dover.

"*Deviation imminent,*" the GPS voice announced in her school-mistressy tone. "Prepare to turn right."

Marie-Dominique steered into the right lane.

"This Boris," she said. "What do you really know about him?"

Where to begin? "I promise you. He would not send us halfway across France without good reason."

But the question rose unbidden at the back of my mind. *Would he?*

J ust off the autoroute, we drifted into the zone of light around an automated tollbooth. Marie-Dominique rolled down a window and fed a credit card into a slot. The cool night air smelled of grass and earth.

As the bar lifted, we glided under it, back into the dark, but now on a different sort of road, no longer a long arm of the order that was Paris. The route narrowed; banks closed in on either side. We were in the country.

In November 1917 this ground saw history's first tank attack as the British flung 476 of its new invention against the German line and overwhelmed it. To the men in their trenches, the turret-less machines grinding across the fields toward them, apparently under no human control, would have looked like ponderous armored slugs, malevolent and alien. Adding to their oddity, each carried a bundle of brush in front, ready to be dropped into a ditch as an improvised bridge.

My own grandfather had been in the Australian Expeditionary Force. He might have been among the infantrymen massed behind the wave of armor, ready to bayonet the German artillerymen in their emplacements and seize their guns. Actions like this left him harmed, a misfit, unable to hold down a job or adjust to life in a country town. It was one of many ways in which I felt connected to France and this ground.

Within half an hour we were entering the outskirts of a town. Dark houses lined the unlit street. Our headlights glinted on a bicycle lying on its side next to an open gate. A cat's eyes flashed as it looked up, startled.

"Well, this is it," said Marie-Dominique. "Bugnicourt. Paris of the Pas-de-Calais."

For a panicky moment, I wondered if Boris really had been playing a practical joke.

But then there were lights, and a barrier, and people.

I f we'd arrived from any other direction, closer to Lille or Cambrai, we'd have seen the small vans and cars pulling trailers that signify a *brocante*. As we pulled up at the tubular steel barrier, two vans drove up on the opposite side, swung off the road into the village, and headed uphill toward the church.

A man in a down jacket and flat cap, cigarette smoking at the corner of his mouth, manned the barricade.

I powered down the window.

"*La Fête du Bœuf?*"

"*Le bœuf en broche?*" The bull on a spit? That sounded near enough.

"*Exact!*"

"Past the church," he said. "At the football field, on the other side of the hill. You can't miss it." He looked at his watch. "They should be starting anytime."

He pulled the barrier aside

On either side of the main street, numbered pitches were squared off in whitewash on the asphalt. Though it was only 3:00 a.m., half were already occupied by people setting up tables and unloading stock: nineteenth-century armchairs, GameBoys, pots and pans, glassware, figurines, hub caps, cooking pots, books, dolls . . . I'd spent uncountable dawn hours in such markets, all over the world, rummaging by the blue-white light of a hissing pressure lamp, alert for the shimmer of antique glass or the dull gleam of silver in the nests of crumpled newsprint.

I felt at home.

Closer to the church, locals had staked out their spots early. Mostly they sold produce. A woman hung skeins of garlic and onions on a rack. Another wrestled a pumpkin from the baby's pushchair in which she'd hauled it from home.

We nosed through a loose crowd of wandering vendors aimless as fish, none in a hurry to get out of the way. From the corner of my eye, I glimpsed men clustered around what looked like a life-size bull, its hide bright blue. A long skirt covered its legs, and a large round hole gaped in the middle of its back.

"Did you see that!?"

"What?"

"Nothing." Who would believe it? I wasn't sure I did myself.

•　　•　　•

On the other side of the hill, there were fewer people. The silence closed in again, broken by the rising howl of a chainsaw biting into wood. Ahead, a glow lit the sky, and we smelled wood smoke.

The football field was alive with light and activity. Tents, striped blue and white, were being raised. The largest filled the lower third of the field, with two smaller ones behind. Others were pitched along the sidelines— mostly stalls, open at the front, for selling things or for games.

Nearest the road, an area was fenced off with permanent wooden rails. Within it, sparks fountained into the air and chainsaws whined. We parked in the shadows and walked across to the rails.

At one end, trees were piled, trunks and branches jumbled together, leafless, the wood weathered, long dead, felled the previous summer and left to season. As two men with chainsaws methodically severed short logs, others with barrows carried them to where flames rose from a slit trench the length of a cricket pitch, its sides lined with steel plates. Directed by two others who patrolled the pit, silently watching the flames, they tossed in the logs, retreating quickly from the heat. Even this far away, it was fierce.

A man leaning on the rail a few meters away said

something to me I didn't hear. When I said, "*Comment?*," he moved closer.

"English?"

"Australian."

"Australia! Have *been* there! Sydney Bridge. *Bière* Fosters." He mimed grabbing a ball under his arm and running. "Rugby"—pronounced "Roog-bee."

He seemed to have summed up my home country pretty well. I nodded toward the flames. "When do they start?"

"Is already one hour burning," he said, pointing to the men cutting and hauling wood. "They fill—then . . ." He made a pressing-down motion with his hands. "Become . . . *cendres*."

Coals. "And after that, how long?"

"Then?" He held up three fingers. Three hours, before the fire was ready.

He nodded toward a smaller tent behind the large one. That must be where they were preparing the animal.

"At six, he come." He grinned. "*Une autre crevette sur la barbecue, huh?*" Even this far from Australia, Paul Hogan and *Crocodile Dundee* had reached their long arm.

Someone called from among the men around the fire pit, and our friend disappeared into the dark.

"What was that about a shrimp on a barbecue?" Marie-Dominique asked.

"Before your time."

We prowled the field, peering into the tents, skirting the steel barriers that cordoned off the small tents where the butchers were at work. For a couple of hours, we dozed in the car, not quite asleep, kept awake by the unrelenting chatter and the chainsaws' howl. When we climbed out again, stiff and disheveled, a crimson sun, fat as a pumpkin, was rising over fallow fields where cows moved uneasily in a white mist.

Chilled, we drifted toward the heat that rippled the air above the fire pit. Of the firewood, only a few branches remained. The rest had fed the bed of coals glowing at near-white heat in the pit. Overnight, supports had been dragged into place at either end: square-section uprights of green-enameled steel, braced from four sides, bolted to wide metal bases, ready to assume the weight. Slots at the top showed where the horizontal beam of the spit would rest.

The big tent was up, sides pulled back as teams of men carried trestle tables inside. It was spacious enough to house a circus, elephants and all. How many people did it take to eat an ox?

There was an atmosphere of the timeless. In another century, people like these—like us—had come here to watch a joust between armored knights, or a hanging, or the burning of a heretic at the stake, or to attend a Mass of celebration and thanks for a great victory, or a carnival, with beer and games and mimed plays, and dancing.

Just then, men turned and looked over their shoulders, laughing.

Marie-Dominique grinned. "Look at this."

It was the blue cow I'd seen in the night. But now the upper torso of a man stuck out of its back, his feet hidden under the skirt. He wore a crimson tunic and waved a wooden sword as he capered awkwardly around the field, defying the solemnity of the moment, playing the fool. If you followed the design of the costume back a few centuries, you'd find the same figure in the world of medieval buffoonery, the Lord of Misrule. A rider in a similar outfit, known as a "hobbyhorse," is part of the team in the English Morris, or Morrish, dances. Further back again and the man would be a real Moor, a North African like those who ruled Spain, and might, but for a few kinks of history, have conquered all of Europe. The farther you left the city behind, the nearer the past became.

Beyond the tents, a tractor engine coughed, then caught and roared in a throaty snarl.

Gushing a plume of exhaust into the cold air, the tractor crawled around the corner of the tent. On two cranked metal arms, lifted high in front of the cab—just as British tanks carried bundles of brush in the battles of 1917—rested the reason for our presence a thousand pounds of flesh and bone.

The metal barriers were pushed back. Nobody spoke as the tractor moved out into the open and jolted toward us over the uneven ground. We who leaned on the railings around the pit, enjoying the heat, stepped back and, in unison, turned toward the approaching machine and its load. There was awe in the air, an awkward reverence. The blue bull ceased his dance and lowered his sword. If he had come to mock the animal at the heart of the event, to brag of our power in vanquishing him, this was not the time.

The indignity of slaughter, of being skinned and gutted, of having head and feet severed, of being spread-eagled between steel grilles and transfixed by the octagonal beam of the spit reduced not a fraction this beast's latent majesty. St Éxupéry was right. "Perfection is achieved, not when there is nothing more to add, but when there is nothing left to take away." This was still the furious adversary matadors faced in the ring, the creature over whom back dancers leaped in the palace of Minos, the animal Picasso drew as the embodiment of maleness, the Minotaur himself.

And we were gathered to devour him.

All our lives we'd eaten meat. But that had been in fragments. To see the animal entire made us aware of our kinship, of a shared nature as creatures of flesh that walked and ate and breathed and bred and died. Here was the true conclusion of my search for the "lost," but it had not gone far enough. What our trivial society has abandoned, and might never retrieve, was what I felt at this moment—awe, and humility, and a profound respect.

Twenty-two

First Catch Your Feast

Man did eat angels' food: he sent them meat to the full.
Psalm 78, King James Bible

A nd then?" Boris asked.

"And then . . . we had lunch."

"Just you and Madame?"

"And about five hundred new friends." I looked around the place where he'd chosen to meet me. "Isn't this a little obvious?"

We were sitting outside a small restaurant on a corner of rue Morillons, in the fifteenth. Across the road, as far as I could see in each direction, stretched the Parc Georges Brassens. Directly opposite, a wide stone gate, its pillars topped by the life-size statues of two bulls, provided an undiplomatic reminder that, from 1894 until the 1970s, these had been stockyards and a slaughterhouse. Deeper inside the park, given less prominence, was a bust of Émile Decroix, the army veterinarian who pioneered what the bust's inscription circumspectly calls *hippophagie*—eating horse, many thousands of which were butchered here.

"I thought it would make you feel at home," Boris said.

"You can joke," I said, "but it was dignified. Even profound."

"You know I don't joke about food. And it isn't necessary to tell me that spit-roasting is an art."

About roasting, he wasn't wrong. At Hampton Court, the palace of Henry VIII, five hundred people did nothing but prepare food. Of these, only four were trusted to roast meat before an open fire. In Escoffier's *brigade de cuisine*, the *rôtisseur* was the equal of its alchemist, the *saucier*. The joint must turn at precisely four rotations a minute to be evenly cooked—the origin of "done to a turn." Other methods had been tried: spit boys who crouched next to the hearth (Henry's priests deplored their nudity); dogs that ran in drumlike treadmills; mechanisms of weights and cogs. None equaled the skilled roaster's experienced eye.

At Bugnicourt, an electric motor rotated the spit at a deliberate five turns to the minute. As fat began to ooze, drops vaporizing in puffs of smoke before they even reached the coals, the rate was raised to six, just enough to stop the dripping.

"They won't really have cooked it by lunchtime?" Marie-Dominique had asked.

"You never roast a whole animal all the way through," I said, recklessly squandering the stock of facts absorbed over a year of reading. "The outside would overcook long before the interior was done."

"Then what are we going to eat?" She was struck by a sudden thought. "We *are* going to eat, aren't we? Because I'm starving already."

"They might carve off the cooked meat and leave the rest to keep roasting," I said. "But I expect they'll butcher the whole carcass and grill the raw meat as steaks."

My guess was right. At 11:00 a.m., the mayor arrived to declare the Fête du Boeuf officially open. Ten minutes later, the tractor returned to lift the beast off the spit and carry it back behind the metal barriers.

At fifteen minutes before noon, a queue was forming outside the tent. We joined it.

And I realized I knew these people. So would anyone who grew up with barn dances in rural town halls, the thump of feet pounding on a board floor; who went to Country Women's Association cake competitions and munched sponges as elastic as foam rubber; who tried not to groan at the annual talent show as a tiny girl wrestled an enormous mother-of-pearl piano accordion through "Lady of Spain." I knew the too-tight collars, the unaccustomed neckties, the tweed jackets Kept for Best, the dresses too elaborate for this time of day (*I told you I didn't have a thing to wear!*). This, for good or ill, was my patrimony, and I surrendered to the experience as one slips under the coverlet of a familiar bed.

Seated on backless benches, eight to a side, at long, bare wooden tables, we drank the aperitif of sweet Cinzano that came with the eleven-euro meal ticket, and read the ads on the paper place mats: the Citroën garage, the farm equipment dealership, the undertaker offering "Funerals at All Prices."

The lady next to me with the unfortunate costume jewelry had driven with her husband from Lille because their son lived nearby and they were going to spend the night at his farm. On my left, a man born in Portugal but working here for twenty years wondered why I was making notes.

"I'm writing a book. About food."

He squinted at me. A writer? So *that's* what they looked like. He supposed someone must write those books that he, he had to confess, seldom read. No, not much of a reader.

"But if it's about food," he said, "why aren't you back there?" He nodded past the stage, in the direction of the smaller tents where they'd taken the carcass.

"I didn't know I could."

He swiveled around on the bench. "Come with me."

We crossed the tussocky grass that, with the tent above and around us, had become a floor. Outside, across a few meters of open space, a dozen men in aprons stood at tables under an open-sided tent and joked as they sliced and hacked and trimmed bloody meat. Off to the side, four women forked steaks from deep plastic dishes and slapped them on barbecues made from oil drums cut in half and filled with coals. The smoke and smell of sizzling meat filled the air. Behind the butchers, discarded, lay what remained of the boeuf: meatless ribs, scraped almost clean, bare as a wreck cast up by the tide.

My new friend knew the butchers, and they knew him. This was a country town. Among 954 people, everyone knows everyone else.

"M'sieur's writing a book. About food. He's from Australia."

"Australia? No kangaroos here, my friend," said one of the butchers. He held up a big fork with a dripping steak impaled. "Only good French beef."

"Kangaroos can be good eating," I said. "The tail, for soup, and the"—what was the word for it? Fortunately Franglais came to the rescue—"*rumsteak*."

"You've eaten it?" one of them asked. Only a couple were working now. We were men talking meat, an important subject. Their subject.

"It's good," I said. "Lean. Like . . . *la venaison*."

They nodded. Interested—until one of the women returned with an empty dish, ready for more steaks.

"Better get on," someone said. "This guy won't cut himself up. Good luck with the book." He nodded toward my Portuguese guide. "Make sure you spell his name right."

A few of the men grinned. My guide must have a reputation for pushing himself forward.

As we walked back, he said, "He was only joking, you know. About the name." A few more steps. "It's Lucas, by the way. From Porto."

A nd was it good?" Boris asked.
    "The best."

I'd been concerned that the beef might be tough, but it was tender and tasty, as good as any I've had in a restaurant. With plastic salad bowls filled with unlimited

The roast

The pit

The butchers

The feast

Marie-Dominique

The leftovers

frites, jugs of a sauce made from the meat juices spiced with whole peppercorns, bowls of sliced baguette, cheese, salad, chocolate mousse . . . not bad for eleven euros.

"And what about the menu for the great *repas*. Is that finished too?"

"Oh, yes. It's done."

I'd mentally compiled it in the car as we drove home that night. I looked forward to eating it one day, sharing the experience with friends as we had shared the ox at Bugnicourt. Sharing was the sauce. The Bible was right. "Better is a dinner of herbs where love is than a stalled ox and hatred with it."

"That calls for a celebration," Boris said. "Let me buy you lunch."

Lunch! A stream of impressions ran through my mind: a crimson lobster claw cracked in the blistering sun of Sète; golden champagne and rose petals on a mountaintop in Provence; dark figs sautéed in spices with a fat duck breast; mussels tasting of pine ash and the sea; the alien perfume of truffle; the forest flavor of fresh girolles; garlic, apples, oysters, chicken, thyme— and beef. The stalled ox where love is.

"Thanks," I said, "I already ate."

The Menu

Aperitif
   Kir royal Florian with confiture of preserved rose petals

Canapés
   Toasts with Gentleman's Relish and halved quail's eggs
   Cucumber sandwiches
   Wine: Vin jaune, or "yellow wine," from the mountainous southeastern region of France, the Jura. Dry sherry, which Jura wine resembles, can be substituted.

Entrée
   French caviar with blinis and crème fraîche
   Wine: A dry champagne, or a white chenin blanc, such as a Savennières from the Loire region

Fish
   Bouillabaisse à l'ancienne

Wine: Continue with the Savennières, or substitute a more robust and aromatic rosé from the Languedoc, around Sète and Marseilles

Meat

Boeuf Bourguignon façon Jean-Christophe

Wine: Traditionally, this dish should be eaten with the same wine as used in the cooking: ideally, a burgundy made from pinot noir grapes. However it's permissible to use a less expensive wine for cooking and a better-quality pinot noir as an accompaniment.

To Refresh the Palate

Sorbet Calvados

Poultry

Guinea Hen à l'Escoffier

Wine: A dry, slightly acid white—Sancerre, Muscadet, Meursault—or a white Beaune such as Puligny-Montrachet

Cheeses

Cheeses of the Auvergne: Cantal vieux, Fourme d'Ambert, Saint-Nectaire

Wine: A lightly sweet and fragrant but robust white, Monbazillac, Riesling, or Gewürztraminer

Dessert

Parfait Swann with baby madeleines

Wine: Continue with the same white as drunk with the cheeses, or return to champagne

Coffee and sweetmeats

Fruits and rose petals *confit* Florian

Digestif

Cognac is the traditional digestif, but if you fancy a change, try Armagnac, a brandy distilled in the Gascony region. In the fourteenth century, Cardinal Vital Du Four claimed that this rich brown spirit "recalls the past to memory, renders men joyous, preserves youth and retards senility. And when retained in the mouth, it loosens the tongue and emboldens the wit." In other words, the perfect lubrication for after-dinner conversation.

Recipes

Kir Royal Florian

Place a coffee spoon of Florian Confiture Pétales de Rose in the bottom of a champagne glass. Add some lychee-based liqueur such as Soho or Lichido to taste, and top up with cold champagne.

Gentleman's Relish

INGREDIENTS

7 ounces anchovies, drained and coarsely chopped

5 ounces butter

2 tablespoons fresh white bread crumbs

¼ teaspoon cayenne pepper

1 dash fresh ground black pepper

1 pinch ground cinnamon

1 pinch freshly ground nutmeg

1 pinch ground mace
1 pinch ground ginger
METHOD
Using a mortar and pestle, pound the anchovies and butter until they resemble a smooth paste. You could also use a food processor. Stir in the bread crumbs, peppers, and spices, and spoon the paste into a large ramekin. Cover and chill before serving.

Bouillabaisse (Serves 4)

There are numerous recipes for this dish, which is best cooked in quantity, for at least a dozen guests, and using whole fish. This recipe is adapted for fewer people and the home kitchen. If you can acquire some shrimp or lobster shells, fish heads, and trimmings, it will improve the flavor and increase the golden color associated with the dish.

INGREDIENTS

3 or 4 pounds raw Mediterranean fish—John Dory, monkfish, snapper. Try to include some oily fish, such as red mullet or mackerel. Avoid salmon and other cold-water fish, which are not typical of the Mediterranean. If you have a good fishmonger, ask him to fillet the fish but give you the bones, heads, and other trimmings.

1 pound raw shrimp in their shells, or a lobster, or both
   (In both cases, frozen whole shrimp or lobster tails
   can be substituted.)

1 cup olive oil

1 teaspoon fennel seed

2 onions, sliced

4 cloves garlic, crushed

4 stalks celery, finely chopped, but with some of the ten-
   derer leaves retained

1 green chili, chopped (optional)

1 bay leaf

3 whole cloves

1 pound ripe tomatoes, peeled and seeded, or 14-ounce
   can chopped tomatoes or pulp

Bottle dry white wine

2 cups water

½ teaspoon powdered saffron or natural saffron strands

Salt and pepper to taste

3 sprigs fresh thyme or ¾ teaspoon dried thyme

METHOD

Cut the fish into large chunks. Remove shells and heads
from shrimp, and shells from lobster tails.

If you are using fish heads, bones, trimmings,
shrimp shells, etc., wrap them in a knotted cloth or piece
of muslin.

Heat the olive oil in a pot large enough for four quarts.

Add the fennel seed. When it begins to brown and pop, add the onion and garlic. Sauté, stirring, until the onion is golden and translucent.

Add the celery, chili, bay leaf, and cloves.

Sauté until the celery is soft.

Add tomatoes, white wine, and water.

(If using) add muslin containing the fish and shrimp heads, lobster shells, trimmings, etc.

Boil at high heat for two minutes, then reduce the heat, and simmer for five more minutes.

(If using) remove the cloth containing the fish heads, shells, etc., and discard.

Add the fish chunks to the broth, with saffron, and salt and pepper to taste.

Simmer only until the fish is cooked through— about three minutes. Even when off the heat, it will continue cooking, so err on the side of too little rather than too much.

Serve in soup plates with plentiful French bread.

Guinea Hen à l'Escoffier

This is Alexandre Gastaud's recipe as it first appeared in the *New York Times*.

*Clean and truss a fat guinea hen weighing one and
a half pounds. Cook it in butter in a saucepan with
a medium-size quartered onion. When the bird is
three parts done, sprinkle it with a teaspoonful of
genuine Rozen paprika and one quarter-pint of
cream (sour, if possible) or with ordinary heavy
cream acidulated by means of a few drops of lemon
juice. Finish the cooking, basting the piece the while
with cream. Dish the bird in a casserole with some
fresh mushrooms tossed in butter and strain over
with the cream. Close the casserole hermetically and
let simmer two minutes before serving.*

NOTES

- Guinea hens, sometimes called *pintades*, are
increasingly available, but a good free-range
chicken can be substituted.
- Saucepans in professional kitchens are larger
than the domestic variety. Home cooks should
sauté the bird whole in plenty of butter in a large
casserole, then cover and pot-roast it until almost
ready to serve (i.e., when a skewer stuck into the
thigh of the bird produces clear juices).
- Rozen, or Rosen paprika, is a Hungarian
paprika from which the seeds and stems have

been removed before grinding. As its main function is to create a pink sauce, any good-quality paprika should serve.

• To "dish" a bird, carve it in the kitchen and bring to the table in a large dish, dressed with the sauce.

(Both the following dishes are the creations of Dr. Nicole Larroumet.)

Sautéed Figs as a Vegetable (Serves 4 to 6)
INGREDIENTS

8–12 ripe but firm figs (2 per person)

Salted butter

½ teaspoon white pepper

½ teaspoon ground nutmeg

½ teaspoon allspice

½ teaspoon ground cloves

Balsamic vinegar

METHOD

Quarter the figs and sauté briefly in plenty of butter, making sure they don't become mushy. When they are warmed through and giving off juices, sprinkle with the powdered spices, turning so that they mix with the butter.

Remove the figs to a warm serving dish and splash balsamic vinegar in the pan to clear the pan's juices. The vinegar will mix with the butter and spices to make a delicious sauce. Pour over the figs. This is excellent as a side dish with roast or grilled duck or pork.

Parfait Swann (Serves 4)

This dessert requires a deep glass for each person. Parfait glasses are preferred; otherwise, use large wineglasses.

INGREDIENTS

1 lemon

1 tablespoon sugar

8-ounce tub Mascarpone cheese

8-ounce tub crème fraîche or sour cream

8-ounce tub thick full-cream "Greek" yogurt

4–6 plain but crumbly cookies—no chocolate chips, raisins, etc.

3 cups fresh raspberries, blueberries, or other small berries in season (In a pinch, use strawberries, but these should be small, or cut into small pieces.)

METHOD

Grate the zest from the lemon and squeeze and save the juice.

Mix lemon juice, lemon zest, and sugar with Mascarpone, yogurt, and crème fraîche or sour cream. Add extra sugar if desired. The mixture should be stiff, not runny. Set aside.

Roughly crush the cookies and place a layer of crumbs about half an inch deep in the bottom of each parfait glass or wineglass.

Add berries until the glass is three-quarters full. (Reserve a berry for each glass as garnish.)

Spoon on cream mixture.

Top with a single berry.

Boeuf Bourguignon
INGREDIENTS

1 cup olive oil

3 pounds good beef—chuck steak, brisket, etc.—in a single piece or large chunks, retaining some fat, cut into 1-inch square chunks

4 large onions, sliced thin

1 clove garlic, crushed

Bottle red wine, ideally burgundy style, made from pinot noir grapes

Bouquet garni (bay leaf, stalk of parsley, two or three sprigs thyme, tied in a bundle)

1 pint beef stock, either fresh or canned (Stock cubes are
   not recommended.)
Salt and pepper
METHOD

Heat half the oil in a deep cast-iron pot.

Sauté the meat in batches, making sure all pieces are well browned. (Do *not* put them in the pot all at once. This will cause them to sweat rather than brown. If they begin to sweat, remove the meat, let the liquid evaporate, add more oil, and commence again, using fewer pieces at a time.)

Lower the heat, transfer the meat to another dish, add the rest of the oil to the pan, and sauté the onion and garlic until browned.

Pour in the wine and bring to a simmer. Stir until all the meat residue on the bottom of the pot is dissolved.

Return meat to pot with *bouquet garni*. Add beef stock (or equivalent amount water) until the meat is barely covered. Season with salt and pepper.

Cover pot tightly with foil, replace lid, and place in the middle of the oven at low heat, about 150 degrees Celsius (300 degrees Fahrenheit).

Cook without unsealing the pot for at least two hours. If, when you check, most of the liquid has not been absorbed and the meat isn't sufficiently tender to be broken up with a fork, replace the seal and cook for another hour. If it seems too dry at any time, add a cup of stock or water, although our aim is a dish with a minimum of liquid.

Unseal, remove *bouquet garni*, skim fat, and serve with simple mashed potatoes and boiled carrots, sliced and sautéed with a little butter and sugar until they begin to caramelize.

Acknowledgments

My gratitude first to my wife, Marie-Dominique, without whom, had she not brought me to France, I would know nothing of great food. Our daughter, Louise, as well as her many treasurable qualities, has become both a skilled cook and a connoisseur of the best in cuisine.

In researching this book, I've been aided by them and by many friends. Christopher Jones was an invaluable companion on some of these hazardous excursions. Charles DeGroot and Dr. Nicole Larroumet offered generous hospitality in Cabris and Bergerac. To Chris Hanley, I apologize for his unfortunate experiences on the Riviera. Thanks are due also to Rick Gekoski; to Peter Grogan, for his advice on wine; to Lauren Sabreau and the staff of Caviar House and Prunier for their cordial welcome; to the administrators of the twenty-third Fête du Boeuf and to the people of Bugnicourt. I also owe a special thanks to the food and vegetable merchants of Paris's sixth *arrondissement* and of the town of Fouras, without whose unfailing maintenance of excellence no good cooking and eating would be possible.

Sincere thanks to my agent, Jonathan Lloyd; my editor, Peter Hubbard; and the entire publishing team at Harper Perennial.

Index

Index